Palgrave Studies in Alternative Education

This series emerges out of a recent global rise of interest in and actual educational practices done with voice, choice, freedoms and interpersonal thoughtfulness. From subversion to introversion, including alternative settings of the state to alternative pathways of the private, the series embraces a diverse range of voices.

Common to books in the series is a vision of education already in existence and knowledge of education possible here and now. Theoretical ideas with potential to be enacted or influential in lived practice are also a part of what we offer with the books.

This series repositions what we deem as valuable educationally by accepting the power of many different forces such as silence, love, joy, despair, confusion, curiosity, failure, attachments as all potentially viable, interesting, useful elements in educational stories. Nothing is rejected if it has history or record as being of worth to people educationally, nor does this series doubt or distrust compelling ideas of difference as relevant.

We wish to allow mainstream and marginal practices to meet here without prejudice as Other but also with a view to ensuring platforms for the Other to find community and understanding with others.

The following are the primary aims of the series:

- To publish new work on education with a distinctive voice.
- To enable alternative education to find a mainstream profile.
- To publish research that draws with interdisciplinary expertise on pertinent materials for interpersonal change or adjustments of approach towards greater voice.
- To show education as without borders or boundaries placed on what is possible to think and do.

If you would like to submit a proposal or discuss a project in more detail please contact: Eleanor Christie Eleanor.Christie@palgrave.com. The series will include both monographs and edited collections and Palgrave Pivot formats.

More information about this series at
http://www.palgrave.com/gp/series/15489

Gina Riley

Unschooling

Exploring Learning Beyond the Classroom

Gina Riley
Adolescent Special Education
Hunter College
New York, NY, USA

Palgrave Studies in Alternative Education
ISBN 978-3-030-49291-5 ISBN 978-3-030-49292-2 (eBook)
https://doi.org/10.1007/978-3-030-49292-2

This Palgrave Macmillan imprint is published by the registered company Springer Nature Switzerland AG
The registered company address is: Gewerbestrasse 11, 6330 Cham, Switzerland

For Ben, my light and my life.
Without you, there would be no me.

Acknowledgments

I gave myself nine months to write this book, because I figured that if a woman can birth a baby in nine months, they could also write a book. The book in your hands is as much my child as any human baby would be. Like raising a baby, this book would not be possible without the help and support of many people.

To my mom, dad, and sister Bernadette—your endless help, encouragement, and love always save the day. I hope I've made you proud.

To my Ben—we did it! Without you, there is no me…but also, without you, there would be no book. You are my whole heart.

To my Bill—you have always been my biggest fan, and I love you so much for that. Thank you for always having my back.

To Dr. Peter Gray—Every time I do research with you, I learn more and more. Thank you for believing in me, and for so graciously allowing me to be a part of your work. I am forever indebted to you.

To my colleagues at the Hunter College School of Education—you make me want to be better and smarter each and every day. You are amazing! To the chairs of my department, past and present, thank you for putting your trust in me, and for giving me work I so love.

To my students—you give me more joy than you can ever imagine. Your dedication to teaching and to your graduate coursework makes me so proud.

To my colleagues within the world of alternative education—thank you for creating a community that is so supportive of one another's work.

Special thanks to Dr. Carlo Ricci, Jerry Mintz, Wendy Priesnitz, Pat Farenga, Laine Liberti, Akilah Richards, Dr. Kevin Currie-Knight, and Blake Boles.

To the late Lisa Heyman, my first unschooling role model. Thank you for supporting me on the path all those years ago.

To Dr. Helen Lees—thank you so very much for believing in me, and for all your help in making this book a reality. I am so very grateful to you.

To Milana Vernikova and Linda Braus at Palgrave Macmillan—so much appreciation for your invaluable assistance and encouragement.

To all those close to my heart who I may not have mentioned, my deepest and most heartfelt gratitude. Soli Deo Gloria

Contents

CHAPTER 1

Introduction

In the year 2001, I made the decision, as a twenty-five-year-old single mother, to unschool my child. It was not a decision I made lightly. Everyone—my parents, my sister, our extended family, the neighbors, expected that my son would, like all the other children in our town, go to school. But he didn't, and no one knew what to do. The choice to homeschool my child, while attending college myself, was a unique one at best…a dangerous one at worst. In other people's eyes, I was conducting a big educational experiment that might not turn out well. In my eyes, I was following my heart and the needs of the beautiful five-year-old boy in front of me.

I needed this book in the year 2001, and I needed a college professor at a traditional school of education to write it. I longed for scientific research on the outcomes of those who had been unschooled. I needed someone who could somehow reassure my family (and myself) that all would be okay, and even better than okay. I wanted assurance that my son would thrive. However, at that time, the research didn't exist.

I did have the support of some friends from La Leche League, and parents from our tiny homeschooling community. I had *Growing Without Schooling*, all of John Holt's books, and later, *Life Learning Magazine*. I remember opening our mailbox and taking out *Growing Without Schooling* once per month and finally feeling like I could breathe. It was nice to know that there were others out there doing the same thing my

G. Riley, *Unschooling*, Palgrave Studies in Alternative Education,
https://doi.org/10.1007/978-3-030-49292-2_1

son and I were doing—living, playing, and learning together, making things work.

During the same time I was homeschooling my son, I was also writing my Master's thesis. Research on homeschooling was just beginning to grow, and it was an exciting time. I wanted to support that research, and also contribute to it myself. My Master's thesis was entitled *An Ethnographic Study on Intrinsic Motivation in Homeschoolers*. I wish I still had a copy. At the time I couldn't afford a computer, so my thesis was typed on a typewriter and given to my thesis committee. It didn't matter. I had a graduate degree, and could finally write Gina Riley, M.S. on my son's quarterly home education reports to the state. Somehow, I thought they would be impressed by this or at least not call Child Protective Services on me for educational neglect, as I now had the same level of education as teachers at our local school. As you can probably tell, the fear around unschooling in the early 2000s was real.

Things got better, both for my son and me, and for the realm of homeschooling. I worked as an adjunct professor at multiple schools, trying to make ends meet. I got married to someone who loved my son (but really didn't understand why he didn't go to school). I started my Ph.D., hoping I could continue to contribute to the research on intrinsic motivation, Self-Determination Theory (Deci and Ryan, 1985), homeschooling, and unschooling. Because of my passion and experience in online education, which was fairly new at the time, I got a job teaching a fully asynchronous online course in Special Education at Hunter College in New York City. I was working, going to school, and homeschooling (really, unschooling) my son.

At Hunter College, I became deeply entrenched in the world of traditional education. My job was to teach teachers. At first, I taught based on what I knew as a psychologist. I focused on the definitions and manifestations of disability. Later on, I would teach classes in testing and assessment. I didn't deeply understand the work of teachers or the challenges they faced in their urban schools, but I tried to teach them all I knew, believing that through our discussions, we would learn and grow together. However, despite really positive evaluations from students, there was an element missing. I did not have experience within New York City schools. As an example, in an evaluation, one of my students wrote:

> I really appreciated Professor Riley's energy and enthusiasm about the topics covered in this course. It seems she is genuinely interested in our

> experiences as teachers and encouraged us to share our daily experiences in the classroom with our peers. However, Professor Riley does seem, to some extent, out of touch with the types of environments and communities that we are working in. She seemed surprised by the types of situations we are dealing with and had few suggestions for how to cope with challenging administrative or familial contexts that our cohort is dealing with on a regular basis. For these reasons, her advice was obviously sound and correct, but not necessarily applicable, and therefore ultimately not as helpful as we'd hoped.

This evaluation was written in 2010 and was absolutely spot on. I loved my teachers but had no idea whatsoever what they were dealing with at their schools. I made a promise to myself to change that, as fast as possible. To be an effective teacher educator, I needed to spend a significant amount of time in traditional schools.

That September, I got a job teaching a sixth and seventh grade math as a leave replacement, continuing my work as an adjunct as well. I spent my weekends attempting to write engaging, differentiated lesson plans. I attended school meetings with colleagues and administration. I saw, firsthand, how the structure of school worked, all while I was also unschooling my child. I loved my math students! They were so patient and kind with me, and seemed to really enjoy the content we were working on (content I had literally learned the day before). However, it was frustrating when we got really into a lesson, and then the bell would ring. It was hard having to follow a strict and rigorous curriculum, when some students really needed time to review the basics of math. It was difficult watching a few students try and fit in with their peers, and seeing peers reject them. Middle school is tough, and we expect pre-teens to just bow to fate and move forward. I knew there was another way to learn and grow, but couldn't obviously share that way with my students. I left the school after a few months. My students wrote me the sweetest cards, saying goodbye.

I still wanted to experience what my teacher candidates went through every day and agreed to take on field supervisory work at middle and high schools in the Bronx, Queens, and Manhattan. I was a field supervisor for years. I got to know different urban schools and their administrators. I loved interacting with the students. I also began to deeply understand the challenges my teacher candidates faced within the average school day, challenges that sometimes felt insurmountable. Some teacher candidates would cry during our post-observation sessions, wanting to help their students but not knowing exactly how. Other teacher candidates understood the system and how it worked, and performed within that structure well.

All this time, I was working on my dissertation, and unschooling my son, who would stay with my parents during the time I was working. My life has always been this odd dichotomy. In the mornings, I would be unschooling alongside my son, learning and experiencing life together. In the afternoons and evenings, I would be observing classrooms and teaching New York City school teachers. I did, and still do, have great respect for both arenas. There are strengths and weaknesses inherent in both the traditional classroom structure and within the unschooling realm. They are both educational choices that need to be supported.

Two years after I received my Ph.D., I received a full-time job as a Clinical Professor of Adolescent Special Education at CUNY Hunter College. I've always wanted to be a full-time academic, and this position was literally a dream come true. I now coordinate the Adolescent Special Education Program at Hunter, and offer traditional and fully online graduate degrees leading to teacher certification in New York State. I love my job, I love my graduate students, and I will do anything and everything to support their work both within their graduate classes and at the schools they teach in. Teaching is the hardest and most valuable work in the world.

I also write, research, and speak on topics related to intrinsic motivation, Self Determination and Cognitive Evaluation Theory (Deci and Ryan, 1985), homeschooling, unschooling, and other alternative learning environments. I have a personal as well as professional motivation to help unschooling become a legitimate educational choice, among a myriad of choices available. This is why it was my dream to write this book.

When I speak, I often get the question: "Don't you think you have some research bias considering your personal positive experience with unschooling?" To that, I answer: "Name me an academic who doesn't have a love for and a personal investment in the topic they study". I find both unschooling and traditional schooling deeply interesting, and honor and support both realms. The satisfaction I get from my work is truly intrinsic.

Thus, I present to you *Unschooling: Exploring Learning Beyond the Classroom*. It is, in many ways, my love letter to the unschooling community. It is also full of critical research about unschooling and self-directed learning. It is the first academic book on unschooling ever written. It is the book I needed and wished for almost twenty years ago.

Chapter 2 contains a description of the history of the unschooling movement, including elements of Rousseau, Dewey, and A. S. Neill's work. A large part of the chapter is dedicated to exploring the work of Ivan Illich and John Holt, and the enormous impact they had on the unschooling movement. Chapter 3 discusses the educational and psychological theories that support the enhancement and utilization of self-directed, intrinsically motivated, multifaceted learning, and reinforce ideas inherent within the philosophy of unschooling. The specific theories discussed in this chapter include Edward Deci and Richard Ryan's Self-Determination and Cognitive Evaluation Theory (1985), John Bowlby's Theory of Attachment (1979), and Howard Gardner's Theory of Multiple Intelligences (1983). Chapter 4 explores the growth of homeschooling, and thus, unschooling.

The second part of the book delves deep into the topic of unschooling. Chapter 5 discusses the basic definition and core philosophy of unschooling and reviews basic demographic data on those who unschool. The spectrum of unschooling is also introduced, and an overview of the three major forms of unschooling is presented. Within Chapter 6, research related to why families choose unschooling is considered. It is clear that in some cases, families choose unschooling after a period of formal schooling, wanting a break from the rigidity and schedule of a traditional school. Other parents move from a period of homeschooling to a more casual unschooling style. Some choose unschooling from the beginning, having been influenced by a particular parenting philosophy, book, or person within the movement.

One of the most common questions asked of unschooling families is "How do children learn if there is no set curriculum?" In Chapter 7, subject-based learning in unschooling is reviewed, including how unschoolers learn to read, do math, gain knowledge of history and science, and acquire proficiency in a second language. Chapter 8 explores the challenges and benefits of unschooling according to the existing research. Challenges examined include feelings of social pressure regarding the decision to unschool, the perceived socialization issue, effects on a parents' time, career, and income, and legal concerns associated with unschooling. Specific benefits discussed include increases in children's learning and intrinsic motivation, increased family closeness, and increased family freedom of schedule.

The last part of the book examines the outcomes of unschooling, different branches of unschooling, and how unschooling has and may continue to influence traditional school structure. Chapter 9 examines grown unschooling outcomes, and includes stories and vignettes from those who have unschooled for all or part of their kindergarten through 12th grade years. Specific outcomes regarding higher education, careers, and financial independence are analyzed and explored. Chapter 10 focuses on different branches of unschooling that have evolved as unschooling has grown in popularity. These branches include Worldschooling, Hackschooling, and Forest or Outdoor Schooling. In the final chapter, the future of unschooling is explored, including how unschooling has and will continue to serve as a model for more traditional schools in the future.

It is my hope that this book provides academics, parents, administrators, and stakeholders within the world of education with the information and research needed to learn about the past, present, and future of the unschooling movement. I also hope that this book assists in adding legitimacy to the notion of unschooling as a viable educational option. We have so much more to learn about the benefits of self-directed, self-determined learning outside of school, and research on unschooling is still in its infancy. I look forward to watching the movement grow, and am honored to be able to be a small part of that growth. Indeed, the history of unschooling is still being written.

References

Bowlby, J. (1979). *A secure base: Parent-child attachment and healthy development*. London: Routledge.

Deci, E. L., & Ryan, R. M. (1985). *Intrinsic motivation and self-determination in human behavior*. New York: Plenum Press.

Gardner, H. (1983). *Frames of mind: The theory of multiple intelligences*. New York: Basic Books.

Growing Without Schooling. (2020). https://www.johnholtgws.com/.

Life Learning Magazine. (2020). http://www.lifelearningmagazine.com/.

CHAPTER 2

Historical Overview of Unschooling

The number of families choosing to homeschool has grown tremendously in the past decade. In 2016, the National Center for Education Statistics reported that approximately 1.7 million students were homeschooled in the United States (McQuiggan, Megra & Grady, 2017) and that number continues to increase (Ray, 2018). As the number of families in the United States and abroad grows, there becomes an increased variety in the ways in which families choose to homeschool their children.

Unschooling is a variation of homeschooling where, instead of following a set curriculum, children learn through everyday life experiences. These experiences are of their choosing and tend to match their strengths, interests, and personal learning styles (Wheatley, 2009). Unschooling is not "school at home." In unschooling, there are no assignments, no set curriculum, and no structured assessments. Within an unschooling environment, parents do not directly teach or provide direct instruction. Instead, they provide an environmental context that supports their child or teen's learning and development (Gray and Riley, 2013). Unschoolers are usually registered by their school districts as homeschoolers. Then, the parent/parents who are homeschooling allow the child to lead their own learning experience (Gray, 2017). The percentage of homeschoolers who consider themselves unschoolers can be estimated at approximately 20%, and that number continues to grow at a steady rate as unschooling increases in popularity (Blanding, 2018).

G. Riley, *Unschooling*, Palgrave Studies in Alternative Education,
https://doi.org/10.1007/978-3-030-49292-2_2

As more families are choosing unschooling, different forms and structures regarding what it means to be unschooled have been created. Radical unschoolers allow their children to completely create their own day; while relaxed homeschoolers may have their children do some form of structured school-based work. Some parents are gathering together to form unschooling cooperatives, or places where families unschool together, uniting skills, strengths, and talents. For those parents who cannot unschool due to time or space constraints, self-directed learning centers allow children and teens to unschool within an adult supervised space.

Hunter-Gatherers

While it may seem that unschooling is a new endeavor, eleven to twelve thousand years ago, hunter-gatherer children were free to play, explore, and learn in their own chosen ways (Gray, 2017). They learned through hunting, foraging, tracking, and through identifying the plants and animals native to their environment. They naturally had to defend themselves against predators. Like all children, they spent lots of time dancing, creating, listening to music, and singing. Hunter-gatherer children would watch their elders performing essential tasks and would learn from that observation. Although elders in hunter-gatherer cultures did not teach their children directly, they were always willing to help the children if they sought help. They also allowed children to join in their activities, even if having the children assist made the activity take longer. Learning occurred through cultural transmission, and took place in trusting, communal contexts. Cultural transmission occurs without formal teaching, and is a way of learning and passing on information through familial or cultural norms (Reber, 1995).

As humans made the steady and perhaps inevitable shift from hunter-gatherer to agricultural societies, the cultural norms of hunter-gatherer communities were replaced with increasingly formal and hierarchical social structures. These hierarchies required a large number of their populations to engage in strenuous and often forced labor for the benefit of their superiors, or the task at hand. This resulted in a significant decline in the amount of time allotted to play and exploration, an unfortunate trend that persisted from its beginnings in the Neolithic Era to the Middle Ages, the Renaissance, and beyond. As advances in literature, philosophy, art, music, astronomy and technology brought about during the Renaissance

Period and Enlightenment began to spread, the concept of hierarchical societies as the only viable means of social organization began to face increasing scrutiny by writers, philosophers, educators, and other notable thinkers (Pai, 2016).

Jean Jacques Rousseau

John Jacques Rousseau (1712–1788) was a philosopher, writer, composer, and a major figure during the Age of Enlightenment. He was particularly close to his father, who imparted a love of reading to him. In his book *The Confessions of John Jacques Rousseau* (1782/2017), Rousseau shared that he had no recollection of actually learning to read, but he remembered how, as a five or six-year-old child, his father encouraged his love of reading:

> Every night, after supper, we read some part of a small collection of adventure stories, which had been my mother's. My father's design was only to improve me in reading, and he thought these entertaining works were calculated to give me a fondness for it; but we soon found ourselves so interested in the adventures they contained, that we alternatively read whole nights together and could not bear to give over until at the conclusion of a volume. Sometimes, in the morning, on hearing the swallows at our window, my father, quite ashamed of this weakness, would cry "Come, come, let us go to bed; I am more a child than thou art. (Rousseau, 1782/2017)

Rousseau imparted his philosophy of education through a fictional and philosophical work entitled *Emile: Or, On Education* (1762/1979). *Emile* is composed of five books. The first three follow Emile as an infant, toddler, and child, learning from his environment, his family, and his beloved tutor. The fourth book explores Emile's learning as an adolescent, also facilitated by his tutor, who dedicates his life to the education of Emile. The fifth and final book outlines Emile's experience as a young adult (as well as highlighting the learning experiences of his female companion, Sophie). In *Emile*, Rousseau tried to demonstrate how children could be brought up having equal feelings and respect for others. He also expressed his philosophy of education, which comprised of three main sources: nature, men, and things. *Emile* is a collection that focuses on the sacredness of childhood, emphasizing that education should be natural, simple, and unstructured. Within the books, learning is seen as a path to discovery, a time to identify interests, and as a way to create individuals who can reason and think critically.

Although *Emile* is seen as one of the first child-centered, progressive works on education, it does have its critics. In 2009, evolutionary psychologist Peter Gray wrote a blog post criticizing Rousseau's work, especially when it came to viewing *Emile* as a treatise on the power of child-centered education. Gray first states that the character of Emile was a protected child, under the care of a tutor that was dedicated to providing an environment that would ensure success. This environment, to Gray, seemed behavioristic and controlling. Rousseau also writes about Emile's learning within distinct, inflexible stages of development, which Gray compares to Piaget's Theory of Cognitive Development (1952). However, the criticism Gray believes as most essential is that, according to Rousseau (and most modern educational theorists), the secret of educational success lies in the intellect and benevolence of teacher and the strength of the environment. Gray disagrees, stating "it does not; it lies in the capacity of children...children educate themselves" (2009). This idea of children educating themselves is something that comes up frequently when discussing unschooling.

Gray is not the only intellectual to disagree with Rousseau. John Dewey, in his book *Democracy and Education* (1916), spends much time criticizing Rousseau's views on education. In particular, although Dewey agrees with Rousseau's thought that nature, men, and things are a large part of the process of learning, these elements are not the only foundations for the acquisition of knowledge (Fennel, 1979).

John Dewey

John Dewey (1859–1952) was an American psychologist, philosopher, academic, and one of the most significant voices in educational reform in the twentieth century. He was also deeply dedicated to individuals becoming socially engaged, democratic citizens. Although he was never a proponent of homeschooling or unschooling, many of his ideas have influenced those who have chosen to unschool. His work *My Pedagogic Creed* (1897/1929), is specifically interesting to look at through an unschooling lens. As an example, in the third paragraph of *My Pedagogic Creed*, Dewey states: "The child's own instincts and powers furnish the material and give the starting point for all education." Immediately one sees Dewey's strong belief in the intrinsic motivation of the learner, outside of traditional school. One of Dewey's most famous quotes, found in Article 2 of *My Pedagogic Creed* states that "I believe that education, therefore, is a process of living, and not preparation for future living." He echoes this idea again in his 1916 work *Democracy and Education*, stating "the very process of living together educates." Dewey explicitly stated that living and learning cannot be separated, something that unschoolers inherently know and experience every day of their lives.

A. S. Neill

A. S. Neill (1883–1973) was a Scottish educator, psychoanalyst, and author who spent much of his life in the classroom. He was highly influenced by the work of Homer Lane (1875–1925), a school superintendent and fellow psychoanalyst who ran a school in Dorset, England called the Little Commonwealth School, which focused on freedom and autonomy for all students (McDonald, 2019a). A. S. Neill founded the Summerhill School in 1921. Summerhill was a democratic boarding school that he described at length in his book *Summerhill: A Radical Approach to Child Rearing* (1960). Neill's daughter, Zoe Readhead, is now principal of the Summerhill School (Gray, 2017). Summerhill is a democratic free school, where attendance at class is optional, and based on student interest in a particular subject. Students are involved in school governance through schoolwide meetings. Neill believed strongly that one's intrinsic interest in a topic or field of study should always be the starting point of all learning, as if something is intrinsically motivating, it signified value and importance to the learner. He also felt that subject-based learning was important, but that a student's personal happiness was even more important, paving the way for later studies on social-emotional learning. At Summerhill, everyone is allowed to do what they want to do unless it encroaches on another person's health, safety, or freedom. Neill's books and philosophies greatly influenced the free school and Sudbury school movements in the 1960s, as well as those who practiced unschooling (mostly underground) in the sixties (Prudhomme and Reis, 2011). His focus on intrinsic motivation in learning, with an emphasis on happiness, imagination, curiosity, and free will during childhood and adolescence, has profoundly influenced the underlying philosophy of the current unschooling movement (McDonald, 2019b).

Ivan Illich

Ivan Illich (1926–2002) was a philosopher, Roman Catholic priest, and critic of modern institutions and practices. Illich's *Deschooling Society*, published in 1971, was a groundbreaking and highly influential critique of compulsory education, and a book that continues to influence many who practice unschooling. In fact, Illich's term "deschooling" is most likely the source of the more contemporary term "unschooling". In *Deschooling Society*, Illich argues that school itself cannot be reformed, but must instead be dismantled and rethought. In the first part of *Deschooling Society*, Illich describes how learning happens, stating that "most learning happens casually, and even more intentional learning is not the result of programmed instruction" (1971, p. 20). He uses second language acquisition as an example. Most children will learn their first language naturally, by listening to others speak. Second language learning tends to be best internalized not by sequential teaching, but instead by cultural transmission. An example of this may be learning from grandparents or living within a different culture.

Illich also proposed the idea of learning from skill models, which is a core feature of most unschooling. As defined by Illich "a skill model is a person who possesses a skill and is willing to demonstrate its practice" (1971, p. 89). Within an unschooling environment, this skill model can be a paid instructor or someone who teaches a skill for no cost or barter. As an example, author and journalist Kerry McDonald, within an episode of the *Learning by Living* podcast, shared the process of gaining a skill model for her daughter, who became interested in Korean language, culture, and history. A skill model was found by putting out an email to her local community unschooling listserv asking for someone who had knowledge of Korean language and culture. Now, Kerry's daughter meets with her Korean language "skill model" three times per week at the local library to practice her language skills (Currie-Knight and Riley, 2019).

In *Deschooling Society*, Illich states that "a good education system should have three purposes" (1971, p. 78). First, it should provide all who want to learn, regardless of age, with access to available resources. Second, it should allow for a place or forum for people who want to share what they know to have access to those who want to learn. Lastly, it should allow those who want to present an issue to the public space to make those challenges known. Those who run unschooling cooperatives have taken note of Illich's words, providing individuals of all ages with access to resources, skill models, and cooperative spaces to learn and grow freely. Those in Sudbury or democratic schooling spaces have also taken Illich's three tenets to heart. Democratic and Sudbury schools offer everything an unschooling cooperative does, as well as a democratic system where students and staff jointly create rules. Sudbury schools also have a system of justice that allows students to report grievances, contest behavior infractions, or bring up issues they may have with school rules or laws.

As maintained in the previous pages, unschooling has deep historical roots that start with hunter-gatherer societies and proceed throughout the ages. However, no one has had more influence on the unschooling movement than John Caldwell Holt. His books, his writings, and his magazine, *Growing Without Schooling* introduced millions to the notion that there is a way to learn, successfully and with great joy, outside of a school environment.

John Holt

John Holt (1923–1985) was an American author and educator. He is also considered the "father of the unschooling movement." He started his career as a teacher who worked in private schools. According to Pat Farenga, John's closest colleague, "John Holt developed a philosophy of education based on his personal observations, reading, experiences, and conversations with children, as well as with adults who did not use grades, bribes, threats, punishment, or other forms of control to make children learn" (Farenga, 2016).

At first, Holt's philosophy of natural learning showed up in his teaching, causing ire in the administration of the schools he taught in. At the same time as he was teaching, he was observing other colleagues' classrooms, the students around him, and his sister's children. He noticed how much learning was going on through play and how children of all ages learn instinctively, without formal instruction. Holt also shifted from promoting free or democratic school models and ideas for school reform to promoting self-directed learning itself (Gaither, 2018).

How Children Fail (1964), Holt's first book, described his life as a teacher and focused on how compulsory schooling negatively affects children's natural curiosity and replaces it with a desire to please the adults around them. *How Children Fail* began a national debate on the quality of schools in the United States, a debate that still exists today (Greer, 1985). In the book, Holt suggested that homeschoolers could provide stakeholders and researchers of education with valuable information regarding how children can be educated in a variety of settings. Holt's second book, *How Children Learn* (1967), compared the informal education children receive in a homeschooled environment with formal education children receive at school and gave recommendations for changing the existing education system to allow more freedom and autonomy, both in how children are educated and where children are educated. Both books have sold over one and a half-million copies, and are must-reads for new unschoolers. In 1968, Holt left teaching to lecture at the Harvard Graduate School of Education and the University of California, Berkeley (Gaither, 2018).

The 1970s created a more radical Holt, and it was in this decade that he shifted his advocacy work from school reform to school liberation for children. He also fought for equal rights for all, including children (Holt 1972; 1976). In *Freedom and Beyond* (1972), Holt discusses the lack of equity and overt classism that exists in schools. He also opens a conversation about what a "deschooled" society would really look like, again stating that there are many paths and places for learning, school being only one of them.

He extended this thought when he wrote *Instead of Education: Ways to Help People Do Things Better* (1976). In this book, he outlines reasons why schools don't work, and explores alternatives to school that do work, based on his experiences with homeschoolers and unschoolers. These alternatives may sound familiar to many experienced unschoolers, but in 1976, they were truly groundbreaking. This included getting rid of school schedules to create personal learning schedules, using community resources such as libraries, playgrounds, and community centers to create learning cooperatives, and taking advantage of free or low-cost museums, concerts, and activities within one's city, municipality, or town.

The mid-seventies also brought the advent of *Growing Without Schooling* (*GWS*), the first newsletter in the United States for homeschoolers and unschoolers, which started official publication in 1977. *Growing Without Schooling* was created by Holt to share ideas and stories about learning outside of school, and formed a sense of community (and a sense of comfort) for those parents and families who decided to educate their child out of traditional school. In true John Holt style, *GWS* was packed to the brim with personal stories of learning outside school, and with resources parents could use to support their choice to homeschool or unschool. He also sometimes inserted the supportive research of sociologists and writers like Margaret Mead and Jean Leidoff, to demonstrate that there were others all over the world learning and thriving without institutional school.

John Holt spent his final years expanding *Growing Without Schooling* with the invaluable assistance of Pat Farenga. He also traveled across the country to speak and secure the legal foundation for those who chose to homeschool or unschool, including making much talked about media appearances on *The Phil Donahue Show* (2015). After Holt's death in 1985, *Growing Without Schooling* continued publication due to the commitment and work of editors Pat Farenga, Donna Richoux, Susanna Sheffer, and Meredith Collins until 2001. *GWS* was a truly instrumental resource for those within the world of self-directed learning and an integral part of John Holt's legacy.

After Holt's death, many others stepped up to carry the torch of the movement. Wendy Priesnitz's home education magazine, *Life Learning Magazine*, took over when *Growing Without Schooling* ceased publication, and became an important resource for unschooling families. As she states in her biography "I believe that children's abilities are grossly underestimated in our society, and that children and young people should be able to live and learn with adults who trust and respect them" (Priesnitz, 2019). Priesnitz's writing can now be found on the Life.ca web domain. Grace Llewellyn was inspired by John Holt's work, and in 1991 wrote *The Teenage Liberation Handbook: How to Quit School and Get a Real Life and Education*, which became an underground hit with parents of teens and adolescents themselves yearning to learn outside of traditional school.

John Taylor Gatto

The nineties were an interesting time for John Taylor Gatto (1935–2018) a New York State and New York City Teacher of The Year who decided to leave teaching after thirty years. He announced his plans in an Op-Ed in the *Wall Street Journal*. He wrote:

> I just can't do it anymore. I can't train children to wait to be told what to do. I can't train people to drop what they are doing when a bell sounds; I can't persuade children to feel some justice in their class placement when

> there isn't any, and I can't persuade children to believe teachers have valuable secrets they can acquire by becoming disciples. That isn't true. (July 25, 1991)

Gatto's pronouncement struck a chord in many people, including parents frustrated with the school system and struggling to find alternatives, school reformers, and teachers trying to find their way in a broken system. If Gatto could quit his job, a job that he was rewarded for being good at, then others could take control of their families' educational choices too. Taking hold of the new opportunities presented to him, Gatto became a sought-after speaker at education, homeschooling, unschooling, and democratic schooling conferences. He expanded on his views in numerous books, including *Dumbing Us Down: The Hidden Curriculum of a Contemporary Society* (1992) and *The Underground History of American Education* (2001), which was considered by some to be his magnum opus (Churchill, 2019).

Peter Gray

In the early 2000s, it was evolutionary psychologist Peter Gray (1946–present) who gave new life, and a research basis, to the unschooling movement. Dr. Gray is an American researcher, evolutionary psychologist, and research professor at Boston College. He is the author of a much-utilized introductory psychology textbook, entitled *Psychology* (2018) as well as the best-selling book *Free to Learn: Why Unleashing The Instinct To Play Will Make Our Children Happier, More Self Reliant, and Better Students for Life* (2013). He is also the author of the popular *Psychology Today* blog *Freedom to Learn*, which focuses on research around play, natural learning, education, and unschooling. Additionally, he is the founder of the Alliance for Self-Directed Education (ASDE), which is dedicated to promoting self-directed learning as a replacement for formal schooling. Dr. Gray has brought a much-needed research-based perspective to the field of unschooling and self-directed learning, and his collaborative studies on unschooling families and young adult unschoolers (Gray and Riley, 2013, 2015; Riley and Gray, 2015) have given legitimacy to a formerly under-researched movement.

The rise of the internet has become an incredible resource for those who are veteran unschoolers, as well as for those seeking information about unschooling. Early listservs became a popular place for questions, inspiring quotes, and support. Lisa Heyman was an early unschooling pioneer who frequently posted on listservs, sharing positive news about unschooling and reassuring parents that they were making a legitimate and important educational choice. Sandra Dodd started an unschooling blog (sandradodd.com) which is still a popular place on the internet for unschoolers and unschooling families. Young adult unschooler Peter Kowalke shared stories about individuals who grew up in the 70s, 80s, and 90s without schooling both online and in print. Sue Patterson started her blog focused on supporting unschooling parents, which is now called unschoolingmom2mom.com. Many other unschooling families started using the internet as a place to write about unschooling, document learning within the home, and find community. The world of unschooling also became an entrepreneur's dream, and created business opportunities for individuals like Blake Boles, an author, speaker, and self-directed learning advocate who now runs the website blakeboles.com; and Jim Flannery, an inventor and engineer best known for creating the Peer Unschooling Network. Neither Boles nor Flannery were unschooled themselves, but have become leaders in the movement due to their enthusiasm and support of self-directed learning environments.

The second decade of the twenty-first century has also created many Facebook, Twitter, Instagram, and YouTube "unschooling experts." Most every unschooler or unschooling family maintains a blog or social media account, and feels safe enough to make their choice to unschool freely known. However, without the work of Rousseau, Dewey, Neill, Illich, and more recently Holt, Gatto, and Gray, unschoolers would still be at the margins of society, in fear of government punishment and societal exclusion. It is important for current unschoolers to understand the history of the movement so that they can forge forward in a way that promotes unification and acceptance within their community and beyond.

References

Blanding, M. (2018, October 2). Twenty percent of home-schooled kids are getting 'unschooled'. What's that? *The Boston Globe*. https://www.bostonglobe.com/magazine/2018/10/02/home-schoolers-turn-boston-area-new-unschooling-centers/j4TB7K54hm7V7ri0yDPTlM/story.html.

Boles, B. (2020). Blakeboles.com. https://www.blakeboles.com/.

Boston College: Morrissey College of Arts and Sciences. (2019). Peter Gray, Research Professor. https://www.bc.edu/content/bc-web/schools/mcas/departments/psychology/people/affiliated-and-emeritus/peter-gray.html.

Churchill, C. (2019, August 10). Churchill: Remembering john taylor gatto. *Times Union*. https://www.timesunion.com/7dayarchive/article/Churchill-Remembering-John-Taylor-Gatto-14291234.php.

Currie-Knight, K., & Riley, G. (2019–Present). *Journalist and parent of four unschoolers: Kerry McDonald*. (No. 3) [Audio podcast episode]. Learning by Living. https://www.spreaker.com/show/learning-by-living-podcast.

Dewey, J. (1916). *Democracy and education: An introduction to the philosophy of education*. New York: Macmillan.

Dewey, J. (1929). *My pedagogic creed*. Washington, DC: The Progressive Education Association.

Dodd, S. (2019). Sandradodd.com. https://sandradodd.com.

Farenga, P. (2016). *The foundations of unschooling*. https://www.johnholtgws.com/the-foundations-of-unschooling.

Fennel, J. (1979). Dewey on Rousseau: Natural development as the aim of education. *The Journal of Educational Thought, 13*(2), 109–120.

Gaither, M. (2018). *John Holt: American teacher and writer*. Encyclopedia Britannica. https://www.britannica.com/biography/John-Holt.

Gatto, J. T. (1991, July 25). I may be a teacher but I am not an educator. *The Wall Street Journal*.

Gatto, J. T. (1992). *Dumbing us down: The hidden curriculum of compulsory schooling*. Philadelphia: New Society Publishers.

Gatto, J. T. (2001). *The underground history of American education: A schoolteacher's intimate investigation into the problem of modern schooling*. New York: Oxford Village Press.

Gray, P. (2008–present). Freedom to Learn. https://www.psychologytoday.com/us/blog/freedom-learn.

Gray, P. (2009, February 12). *Rousseau's errors: They persist today in educational theory*. Freedom to Learn. https://www.psychologytoday.com/us/blog/freedom-learn/200902/rousseau-s-errors-they-persist-today-in-educational-theory.

Gray, P. (2013). *Free to learn: Why unleashing the instinct to play will make our children happier, more self-reliant, and better students for life*. New York: Basic Books.

Gray, P. (2017). *Self-directed education—Unschooling and democratic schooling*. Oxford Research Encyclopedia of Education.

Gray, P., & Bjorklund, D. F. (2018). *Psychology* (8th ed.). New York: Worth Publishers.

Gray, P., & Riley, G. (2013). The challenges and benefits of unschooling according to 232 families who have chosen that route. *Journal of Unschooling and Alternative Learning, 7*(14), 1–27.

Gray, P., & Riley, G. (2015). Grown unschoolers' evaluation of their unschooling experiences: Report I on a survey of 75 unschooled adults. *Other Education, 4*(2), 8–32.

Greer, W. R. (1985, September 15). John Holt, author and educator, dies at 62. *The New York Times*. https://www.nytimes.com/1985/09/15/us/john-holt-author-and-educator-dies-at-62.html.

Growing Without Schooling. (1977–2001). https://www.johnholtgws.com/growing-without-schooling-issue-archive.

Growing Without Schooling. (2015). John Holt on the Phil Donahue Show discussing unschooling [Video]. YouTube. https://www.youtube.com/watch?v=fXLWPpln0rQ.

Holt, J. (1964). *How children fail*. New York: Pitman Publishing Company.

Holt, J. (1967). *How children learn*. New York: Pitman Publishing Company.

Holt, J. (1972). *Freedom and beyond*. New York: Dutton.

Holt, J. (1976). *Instead of education: Ways to help people do things better*. New York: Dutton.

Holt, J., & Farenga, P. (1977–2001). *Growing Without Schooling*. https://www.johnholtgws.com/growing-without-schooling-issue-archive.

Illich, I. (1971). *Deschooling society*. New York: Harper & Row.

Kowalke, P. (2019). https://www.peterkowalke.com/about/.

Llewellyn, G. (1991). *The teenage liberation handbook: How to quit school and get a real-life education*. Eugene, OR: Lowry House.

McDonald, K. (2019a). *Unschooled: Raising curious, well educated children outside of the conventional classroom*. Chicago, IL: Chicago Review Press.

McDonald, K. (2019b, July 9). *Unschooling: Shifting from force to freedom in education*. https://www.cato-unbound.org/2019/07/08/kerry-mcdonald/unschooling-shifting-force-freedom-education.

McQuiggan, M., Megra, M., & Grady, S. (2017). *Parent and family involvement in education: Results from the National Household Education Surveys program of 2016*. Washington, DC: The National Center for Education Statistics.

Neill, A. S. (1960). *Summerhill: A radical approach to child rearing*. New York: Hart Publishing Company.

Neill, A. S. (2018). Encyclopedia Britannica. https://www.britannica.com/biography/A-S-Neill.

Pai, A. (2016). Free to learn: why unleashing the instinct to play will make our children happier, more self-reliant, and better students for life [Review of the book *Free to learn: Why unleashing the instinct to play will make our children happier, more self-reliant, and better students for life*, by Peter Gray]. *Evolutionary Educational Outreach, 9*(1).

Patterson, S. (2019). Unschoolingmom2mom. https://unschoolingmom2mom.com/.

Piaget, J. (1952). *The origins of intelligence in children.* New York, NY: International Universities Press.

Priesnitz, W. (2019). Wendy Priesnitz Bio. https://www.life.ca/wendy/.

Prudhomme, M. A., & Reis, G. (2011). Comparing A.S. Neill to Rousseau, appropriate? *Journal of Unschooling and Alternative Learning, 5*(10), 1–19.

Ray, B. (2018, April 20). *Homeschooling growing: Multiple data points show increase 2012–2016 and later.* National Home Education Research Institute. https://www.nheri.org/homeschool-population-size-growing/.

Riley, G., & Gray, P. (2015). Grown unschoolers' experiences with higher education and employment: Report II on a survey of 75 unschooled adults. *Other Education, 4*(2), 33–53.

Reber, A. S. (Ed.). (1995). *The Penguin dictionary of psychology* (2nd ed.). New Jersey: Penguin Press.

Rousseau, J. J. (1762/1979). *Emile: Or, On education.* New York: Basic Books.

Rousseau, J. J. (1782/2017). *The confessions of Jean Jacques Rousseau.* http://www.gutenberg.org/files/3913/3913-h/3913-h.htm.

Wheatley, K. (2009). Unschooling: An oasis for development and democracy. *Encounter, 22*(2), 27–32.

CHAPTER 3

Theoretical Perspectives

As defined in Chapter 2, unschooling is a variation of homeschooling where instead of following a set curriculum, children learn through everyday life experiences. These experiences are of their own choosing, and are not curriculum or lesson-dependent (Gray and Riley, 2015). Although it is John Holt who devised the term unschooling in the 60s and Ivan Illich who called to de-establish school in the 1970s, many more recent educational and psychological theories support the enhancement and utilization of self-directed, intrinsically motivated, multifaceted learning. These theories include Edward Deci and Richard Ryan's Self-Determination and Cognitive Evaluation Theory (1985), John Bowlby's Attachment Theory (1979), and Howard Gardner's Theory of Multiple Intelligences (1983).

Self-Determination and Intrinsic Motivation

According to Ryan and Deci (2000), intrinsic motivation is an innate concept. It is an energy orientation, a display of the positive attributes of humanity which include curiosity, vitality, and self-determination. It is the opposite of extrinsic motivation, which is the desire to engage in behavior for external reasons (Lepper et al., 2005). The concept of intrinsic motivation can be understood within the theoretical framework of Deci and Ryan's (1985) Self-Determination Theory (SDT). As Ryan and Deci (2017) state, "Intrinsic motivation is clearly a manifestation of our natural

G. Riley, *Unschooling*, Palgrave Studies in Alternative Education,
https://doi.org/10.1007/978-3-030-49292-2_3

human propensity to assimilate and integrate knowledge. Characterized by curiosity and interest, intrinsic motivation represents the prototype of an active and willing acquisition and integration of knowledge" (p. 354).

Intrinsic motivation creates a different environment for learning. Instead of learning because they have to, children learn because they want to. John Holt, the American educator and theorist who coined the term unschooling and popularized this form of education beginning in the 1960s, has said that in children, "learning is as natural as breathing" (Holt, 1967). However, in the average public or private school, this is not the case. Students are enticed to learn, not for intrinsic interest, but for A's, praise, and stars. Positive behavior is rewarded, and negative behavior is punished or ignored. Of course, extrinsic rewards can temporarily change behavior and create compliance, but it is intrinsic motivation that is the best predictor for high and long-lasting achievement (Kohn, 1993, 1999, 2018). Within the unschooling environment, children learn through their everyday life experiences and are in control of their own education (Gray and Riley, 2015). It is the ultimate form of self-determined, intrinsically motivated learning.

Self-Determination and Cognitive Evaluation Theory

Although researchers point to intrinsic motivation as an inherent quality, the maintenance and enhancement of this motivation is dependent on social and environmental conditions surrounding the individual (Ryan and Deci, 2000). Deci and Ryan's Cognitive Evaluation Theory (CET) specifically addresses the social and environmental factors that facilitate versus undermine intrinsic motivation and point to three significant psychological needs that must be present in the individual in order to foster self-motivation. These needs are competence, autonomy, and relatedness (1985).

Competence

Unschooling families generally facilitate intrinsic motivation, most times unknowingly, by using Cognitive Evaluation Theory as a basis for their lifestyle. According to Deci and Ryan (1985), a sense of competence comes from success experiences and overall positive feelings about activities, and fosters feelings of intrinsic motivation. Children, by nature, are driven by a need for competence (Deci and Ryan, 1985). Young children will often experiment with and manipulate objects around them, and the joy on their faces when they figure it all out is demonstrative of intrinsic satisfaction (Holt, 1964). Imagine a child who puts together their first puzzle, or a teen that finally solves a Rubik's Cube. Success is sweet! These same individuals will also test their knowledge by assimilating concepts they have already mastered with new stimuli, creating personal challenges for themselves (Piaget, 1952). A sense of competence and the ability to take on optional challenges all foster the development of intrinsic motivation (Ryan and Deci, 2000). Levin-Gutierrez discusses the intertwining concept of competence and challenge in unschoolers using her daughters' interest in the computer game Minecraft. She states: "As my daughters continue to build their way around the Minecraft game, they share with me how the previously uninhabited island has attracted more builders and developed a town. The need for shops, museums, and gardens has grown…and it is up to them to build them" (2015, p. 38). In this example, through a computer game, a sense of true competence has been found.

More broadly, competence is facilitated within an unschooling environment because those who are unschooled have more unstructured time to explore talents and interests. Generally, more time exploring interests equals greater competency developed in these areas (Gray and Riley, 2013). We see this frequently in the number of young actresses, actors, musicians, environmentalists, and artists that were or currently are unschooled. Billie Eilish, a recent five-time Grammy Award-winning musician, is a contemporary example. Eilish's parents state that their children were unschooled partially because, as parents, they were influenced by the homeschooled musical group Hanson. "I was completely swept away by these kids…. clearly what had happened was they'd been allowed to pursue the things they were interested in" (Coscarelli, 2019). Many unschooled musicians, artists, or creatives will share a similar story. They gained mastery in their field because of the amount of unstructured time they had to practice and experiment with their instruments or art forms.

Autonomy

According to Deci and Ryan (1985), in order for intrinsic motivation to flourish, a sense of competence must also be accompanied by a sense of autonomy. When an individual is given a sense of choice, an acknowledgment of feelings, or an opportunity for self-direction, feelings of intrinsic satisfaction are enhanced (Ryan and Deci, 2017). In Gray and Riley's 2015 study, grown unschoolers were asked what they perceived as the greatest benefit of being unschooled. Ninety-five percent mentioned advantages coded as "Time to Pursue One's Own Interest" and "Freedom and Independence." Unschooling is also sometimes termed "autonomous learning," due to the freedom inherent within the unschooled environment (Parkes, 2016). An example of this freedom is found in the daily life of an unschooler. Imagine waking up every day with the ability to freely decide how your time will be spent. Sandra Dodd, an author and parent of grown unschoolers, calls these typical unschooled days "the best ever Saturday...the day people dream about when they are not in school" (Sizer, 2012). One can find many examples of these unscheduled days when reading blogs or books about unschooling families. Although unschooling families sometimes focus their energy on creating choices and opportunities for self- directed learning, they also tend to allow for blissfully unscheduled days, allowing a child or adolescent to spend time exactly as they choose.

Creating choice and opportunities for self-direction is one of the many ways in which unschooling parents provide autonomy support; thereby enhancing a student's intrinsic motivation (Deci et al., 1991; Ryan and Powelson, 1991). Autonomy support can be created by providing an environment that values an individual's freedom, offers meaningful choices, uses non-controlling language and actions consistently, and unconditionally accepts internal motivations (Nunez and Leon, 2015). As one participant in Gray and Riley's (2015) study of young adult unschoolers shared:

> My parents created an open, supportive environment for my brother and me. They shared their interests with us, brought books and movies and experiences into the house, and let us move at our own pace....When we began unschooling, my parents let go of their self- imposed responsibility for my education - they had confidence in my ability to organically learn what I needed. (p. 17)

Relatedness

Autonomy support and relatedness go hand in hand, as both needs influence the cognitive and affective outcomes of education (Deci and Ryan, 2009; Ryan and Powelson, 1991). Researchers have specifically stressed that parents who are more involved with their children have children who are more highly motivated and self-directed (Deci et al., 1991; Ratelle et al., 2005; Vallerand et al., 2008). An individual's intrinsic motivation is more likely to flourish when they are feeling a sense of security and relatedness. A sense of relatedness should not only occur during infancy, toddlerhood, or childhood. In truth, relatedness tends to be especially important through adolescence and young adulthood.

Deci and Ryan (2009) state that relatedness is based upon "interpersonal affiliation, authentic care and the sharing of enriching experiences" (p. 570). In individuals who are unschooled, this affiliation tends to be strong, even through the teen years (Gray and Riley, 2013, 2015). Specifically, one of the great benefits of unschooling, according to families who unschool, is the increase they observe in relatedness and feelings of family closeness. As one parent expressed in Gray and Riley's study:

> Hands down, the relationship with our kids has flourished. We have never gone through the typical teen angst or rebellion so often touted as normal. I don't think it is. If you build up your family life where members work together and help one another, where the focus is on happy learning, it's hard NOT to get along and enjoy each other's company! (2013, pp. 16 and 17)

Researcher Elena Piffero (2020), discusses the transformation in household relationships once her family decided to unschool:

> Taking our responsibility for the education and training of our children in full has also forced us to reconsider the type of relationship we wanted to have with (our children), and each other. In fact, we are acutely aware that it is precisely in the family that internal patterns of behavior and action are internalized which will condition them throughout life. Spontaneous learning is based on respect for each individual's needs and competences.... Unschooling is an educational philosophy that favors collaboration and solidarity, removes adult figures from the pedestal of the last repositories of knowledge, and restores dignity, rights and action to the protagonists of learning, the children. (p. 6)

In Billie Eilish's family, a sense of relatedness is key to her success. Songs are written, produced, and performed by herself and her brother (who opens for her concerts and plays her backing track). Most of her recordings are created in her bedroom, not far from her parents, who have been at her side the whole time (Coscarelli, 2019). Unschooling families are particularly practiced when it comes to relatedness because they spend so much time together. More time spent together equals more time learning how to work together, growing alongside each other. Numerous unschooling families have espoused the benefits of increased time learning about each other, noting that when a child is in school, some of that time is erased due to the amount of time children spend in the classroom, or engaging in school-based activities like homework (Gray and Riley, 2013). Schools can take note of this and review their policies on homework and additional school-based responsibilities, in order to assist in supporting the growth of authentic relationships outside of school.

Attachment Theory

Some may immediately recognize that the roots of relatedness come from Bowlby's (1979) theory of infant attachment. According to Bowlby, an infant's intrinsic motivation to learn about the world is more evident when the infant shows a secure attachment to their parent or parents. By allowing a child to balance their attachment needs with the need to explore, a parent is paving the way for later development of self-esteem, self-concept, and competence (Moss and St. Laurent, 2001). Although Bowlby's theory of infant attachment is a bit different from what William Sears terms attachment parenting (2001), researchers have noticed a relationship between attachment parenting as defined by Sears and later unschooling. This relationship also surfaces when reviewing the number of individuals who found out about unschooling through La Leche League, a breastfeeding support organization that endorses attachment parenting as part of their core philosophy (Small, 1999). Sears' definition of attachment parenting includes techniques such as extended breastfeeding, babywearing, and co-sleeping (2001).

Much research has been done regarding the relationship between unschooling and attachment. Donna Kirschner's (2008) ethnographic doctoral dissertation on the unschooling movement noted that the unschooling lifestyle commonly included a history of attachment parenting. Rebecca English's study of unschooling families in Australia (2015) concludes that there is indeed a link between attachment parenting and the decision to unschool one's children. In Gray and Riley's large-scale study of 232 unschooling families, attachment parenting was mentioned as one of the major paths to unschooling (2013).

In 2018, I completed a small qualitative study on the possible relationship between attachment parenting (as defined by William Sears) and unschooling. Twenty-four unschooling mothers between the ages of 24 and 51 responded to the call for research. Nineteen out of those twenty-four mothers believed that there was a link between attachment parenting and unschooling. When asked the question: "Did your experience attachment parenting lead to or influence your decision to unschool?", over half the respondents said yes. Many stated that they believed unschooling was an extension of attachment parenting. One participant felt strongly that unschooling was an organic next step after attachment parenting:

> I've seen it said before that you might not want to attachment parent if you are going to send your children off to school. I think it would be like pulling the rug out from under them. It would be like saying 'I trusted you to be you and fully support you until you reached this arbitrary age of 5 and now I am done with that'. One just flows into the other so naturally.

Another parent expressed that "Yes, I believe that unschooling is a natural extension of attachment parenting and gentle parenting. The underlying idea is that children will thrive with connection and meeting their individual needs." Other parents agreed, stating "Many of the online resources that I accessed for information about attachment parenting included or linked to information about unschooling. It just seemed like a common sense extension of the philosophy of attachment parenting." One parent stated, "I can imagine both come largely from wanting our children to retain their connectedness to self, to other humans, to us, and to the earth."

The Myth of Attachment

The myth regarding attachment parenting (and unschooling) is that both equal a child who is sheltered from the world's ills, disappointments, and dangers. Many times, this is exactly the opposite. One can be healthily attached to a parent or caregiver and still be an autonomous human being. For instance, some of those who unschool and practice attachment parenting also follow what Lenore Skenazy has termed free-range parenting (Callaraco, 2018). Free-range parenting, by definition, is raising children in a way that celebrates the child's personal autonomy and freedom while also taking into consideration developmental age and stage. In 2008, author and speechwriter Lenore Skenazy wrote a controversial column for the *New York Sun* entitled *Why I let my 9 year old son ride the subway alone*. This column was the start of a national free-range parenting movement, and statewide free-range parenting laws. It also led to the formation of the nonprofit Let Grow, whose mission is to lead child independence initiatives at schools, at home, and within communities (2019).

Although in theory free-range parenting seems contrary to attachment parenting itself, in practice, it is not. Indeed, Bowlby, within his attachment theory, stated that in healthy attachment, the parent becomes the child's secure base. That does not mean the child never leaves the parent's side. Instead, when the child is developmentally ready, the child will independently leave the secure base and test their wings, knowing that they always have a safe, unconditional space to go back to when needed (Bowlby, 1979). Depending on age, this autonomous action may bring the child or adolescent to a different playground, a new neighborhood, an unexplored town, or a country overseas.

Gardner's Theory of Multiple Intelligences

Within mainstream society, the age of five marks an important period in a child's life. At the age of five, most children (and parents) prepare themselves for their child to leave the home, most frequently in a space called kindergarten. In kindergarten, it is expected that the child learns skills such as reading, writing, and basic math. It is also the child's entrance into a world filled with content, curriculum, and standardized testing. As stated by Howard Gardner, developmental psychologist and retired Professor of Cognition and Education at the Harvard Graduate School of Education:

> During the first years of life, youngsters all over the world master a breathtaking array of competencies with little formal tutelage. They become proficient at singing songs, riding bikes, executing dances, keeping scrupulous track of dozens of objects in their home, on the road, or along the countryside. In addition, though less visibly, they develop powerful theories of how the world works and how their own minds work...Somehow, the natural, universal, or intuitive learning that takes place in one's home or immediate surroundings during the first years of life seems an entirely different order from the school learning that is now required throughout the literate world. (1991, p. 2)

Even experienced kindergarten teachers agree that we may be rushing things by creating curriculum-based goals for five-year-olds. Expecting children to read by the end of kindergarten may lead to an "upper hand" in first grade, but by concentrating on reading, math, and other academic skills, children in kindergarten are losing the time they need to play. Play is more than fun. It also promotes positive social skills, problem-solving skills, language development, spatial thinking, and allows children time to draw inferences and conclusions. In addition, pushing students to read or practice formal math earlier has not translated to increased test scores or higher overall academic achievement in the United States (Curwood, 2020), thereby putting more stress on teachers and very young students without noticeable quantitative gains.

Gardner recognizes that the early focus on academic achievement and "one-size-fits-all" approach prevalent in how schools teach and assess may not be the real way that children learn and gain understanding, and many seem to agree (Curwood, 2020; Gray, 2019; Kohn, 2001; Jacoby, 2010). He also expresses that "genuine understanding is most likely to emerge, and be apparent to others, if people possess a number of ways of representing knowledge of a content or skill and can move readily back and forth among those forms of knowing" (1991, p. 13). Play is one way to create genuine understanding, but another way is to acknowledge and appreciate the idea that children learn in different ways, and have varied types of inherent strengths and powers. Thus, Gardner introduced his Theory of Multiple Intelligences.

In his theory, Gardner states that intelligence is more than the verbal and spatial intelligence measured by the traditional IQ test, and prized by traditional schools. Instead, there are eight (and possibly nine) different intelligences that account for the diverse ways that children learn and understand the world around them. These intelligences are linguistic intelligence, musical intelligence, logical-mathematical intelligence, visual-spatial intelligence, bodily-kinesthetic intelligence, interpersonal intelligence, intrapersonal intelligence, and naturalistic intelligence. In later years, Gardner mentioned the idea of existential (or spiritual) intelligence (1999).

Linguistic intelligence, according to Gardner, is seen in those who have a particular penchant for all facets of language, including the study of grammar, vocabulary, semantics, phonology, and syntax. Those who show linguistic intelligence may be poets, writers, linguists, and translators. They usually love to read, write, and study the nuances of one language or of different languages (1983). Within this book, you will read many examples of unschoolers who feel a natural propensity toward the learning and mastery of different languages, as well as others who have demonstrated their linguistic intelligence by spending time writing books or collections of poetry.

Those with musical intelligence demonstrate their skill by practicing, performing, and composing music. They study pitch, rhythm, and theory; and may be called to explore the evolutionary, neurobiological, or ethnographic history of music. They gain expertise on an instrument, or a variety of instruments, or may use their own voice as an instrument, possibly as a primary means of creating music. In his book *Frames of Mind: The Theory of Multiple Intelligences*, Gardner expresses that "except among children with unusual musical talent or exceptional opportunities, there is little further musical development after the school years begin" (1983, p. 109). He attributes this to the fact that "music occupies a relatively low niche in our culture, and so musical illiteracy is acceptable" (1983, p. 109). This ignorance of the power of musical intelligence is seen in public and private schools across the country, where music and art classes are the first to be cut when school budgets tighten.

Logical-mathematical intelligence is seen in those who have deep understanding regarding the interconnections between objects in the world, and a specific penchant toward numerical and mathematical structures and concepts. Those with logical-mathematical intelligence may be mathematicians who study numbers, mathematical functions, algebra, calculus, equations, theorems, and problem-solving. Or, they may be math teachers or professors who teach the beauty of numbers to their students (Gardner, 1983). They may also be computer scientists, webmasters, or coders with an attraction to particular STEM (Science, Technology, Engineering, or Math) fields.

According to Gardner, "central to spatial intelligence are the capacities to perceive the visual world accurately, to perform transformations and modifications upon one's initial perceptions, and to be able to recreate aspects of one's visual experience" (1983, p. 173). Spatial intelligence is seen particularly in landscapers, engineers, architects, sculptors, artists, professional chess players, scientists, and comparative psychologists. Gardner espouses the idea that spatial intelligence may improve with age, and can be strengthened by playing chess or checkers, drawing, building with blocks, or experimenting with spatial tasks and puzzles

(1983). These are many of the same tasks that educators have been asked to do less of in their classrooms during the early years of formal schooling.

Bodily-kinesthetic intelligence is observed in athletes, dancers, mimes, martial arts experts, actors, and musicians. Gardner sees bodily-kinesthetic intelligence not as an isolated intelligence, but as a culmination of other intelligences, particularly logical-mathematical intelligence and spatial intelligence (1983). Although famous athletes, dancers, and performers are prized in the United States, we tend to think of sports, dance, martial arts, and theater as "extra-curricular," or things that should happen outside of the school day. This attitude affects the way arts and sports, much like music, is seen in our culture and particularly within our schools. They are topics to explore "on the side," after the more important work of learning core subjects is completed. In contrast, many unschoolers have reported that having autonomy in the way they spent their time gave them hours to pursue and master talents within the realms of arts, theater, music, and sports (Gray and Riley, 2015).

Gardner defines two personal intelligences, which he categorizes as interpersonal intelligence and intrapersonal intelligence. Intrapersonal intelligence can be explained as knowing oneself well, and interpersonal intelligence is about having the innate ability and curiosity to know others well. "In an advanced form, interpersonal intelligence permits a skilled adult to read the intentions and desires....of many other individuals" (Gardner, 1983, p. 239). Those with good interpersonal skills would have the potential to be strong therapists, counselors, social workers, or teachers. Intrapersonal intelligence is especially prized in schools today, mostly because of an increased focus on enhanced social-emotional learning in students. Intrapersonal intelligence is also essential to form a mature sense of self so that one can be successful at home, in the workplace, and in forging intimate relationships with others. Many unschoolers have identified that unscheduled time inherent in unschooling gave them more time to figure out who they were, what they believed in, and what they wanted from life; alluding to an enhanced form of intrapersonal intelligence (Riley, 2018).

Naturalistic intelligence is the last of the original eight multiple intelligences, and refers to those individuals who have an innate interest in the natural world or the environment. Biologists, zoologists, urban planners, foragers, nature educators, park rangers, and anthropologists generally have strong naturalistic intelligence. So do children and teens who are particularly interested in the environment and natural world (Gardner, 1993). The environmental advocate and Nobel Peace Prize nominee Greta Thunberg would be identified as a young person with strong naturalistic intelligence. Interestingly, she is also an adolescent who has skipped lots of school so she can travel around the world and speak about climate change and the environment (Bershidsky, 2019).

In his writings, Gardner has mentioned a ninth intelligence, which he terms existential intelligence. Existential intelligence refers to the ability to tackle deep questions about human existence, such as "why are we here?", "what is the meaning of life?" and "why do we die?". It is a type of philosophical and metaphysical intelligence (Gardner, 1999). This intelligence has been observed in members of religious orders, yogis, rabbis, spiritual leaders, and mystics.

It is important to note that Gardner says nothing about unschooling or self-directed learning explicitly within his theory and has shared that he does not see a natural connection between his writings and the self-directed learning movement (Howard Gardner, personal communication, February 14, 2019). However, he does agree that schools are failing to live up to their mission and need support in understanding how children intuitively learn and think (Gardner, 1991). Some public and private schools have taken this criticism to heart, and have tried to implement a multiple intelligence-based approach in their classrooms by increasing the use of field trips, project-based learning, and art or music-based learning (Abeles, 2016). Unfortunately, many times this attempt is half-hearted and forgotten once standardized test season occurs. It truly is the unschooled environment which matches with Gardner's philosophy that children learn and are intelligent in all sorts of ways and that learning through life is an essential aspect of authentic education.

Unschooling and Cultural Transmission

Within the unschooling environment, much learning comes from cultural transmission, or the sharing of knowledge from one generation to another. This knowledge is born of attachment, intrinsically motivated, and usually is imparted through varied forms of intelligence (not just focused on language or math). Think of a father teaching his daughter about a car engine, or a grandmother teaching her grandson how to cook. As reviewed in Chapter 2, cultural transmission has occurred throughout the entirety of human history. Some may believe that in our current society, elements of cultural transmission have been lost (Neufield and Mate, 2004). Instead of guidance and mentoring coming from trusted or related adults, guidance and mentoring is seen as coming primarily from peers, teachers, and school counselors. Instead of allowing students the time and space to see the innate connections between the different types of knowledge they gain, teachers aim to impart knowledge with direct instruction and curriculum-based goals and objectives, within the time restriction of a forty or fifty-minute period.

Recently, however, it seems that society is fostering a resurgence of the idea of familial and cultural transmission, hence a renewed interest in intergenerational socializing and intergenerational housing (Halpert, 2018). Children and teens, both schooled and unschooled, are spending more time in nursing homes and senior citizen centers reading to, cooking with, and entertaining older adults. Senior citizens are spending more time with the younger generation, talking with and sharing information about their experiences living in a different decade or era. While unschooling can be defined as learning through life, maybe it can also be defined as intergenerational education, as those who unschool frequently learn from the generations before them in a myriad of different contexts and ways.

Unschooling and the Importance of Theoretical Perspective

As an increasing number of families are choosing to unschool, it is essential to further study the workings of this philosophical and educational movement. It is also crucial to ascribe theory to the movement, to gain greater understanding of its workings as well as to increase the legitimacy of unschooling itself. The unschooling environment tends to provide space for self-directed and intrinsically motivated learning, and has deep roots in Deci and Ryan's Self-Determination and Cognitive Evaluation Theory (1985), Bowlby's Attachment Theory (1979), and Gardner's Theory of Multiple Intelligences (1983). Intrinsically motivated, self-directed, multiple intelligence-based learning truly seems to be the future of education itself.

References

Abeles, V. (2016). *Beyond measure: Rescuing an overscheduled, overtested, underestimated generation*. New York: Simon & Schuster.

Bershidsky, L. (2019, June 18). Greta Thunberg's other lesson is about school. *Bloomberg Opinion*. https://www.bloomberg.com/opinion/articles/2019-06-18/greta-thunberg-s-other-lesson-is-about-compulsory-school.

Bowlby, J. (1979). *A secure base: Parent-child attachment and healthy development*. London: Routledge.

Callaraco, J. M. (2018, April 3). Free range parenting's unfair double standard. *The Atlantic*. https://www.theatlantic.com/family/archive/2018/04/free-range-parenting/557051/.

Coscarelli, J. (2019, March 28). Billie Eilish is not your typical 17 year old pop star. Get used to her. *The New York Times*. https://www.nytimes.com/2019/03/28/arts/music/billie-eilish-debut-album.html.

Curwood, J. S. (2020). *What happened to kindergarten?* https://www.scholastic.com/teachers/articles/teaching-content/what-happened-kindergarten.

Deci, E. L., & Ryan, R. M. (1985). *Intrinsic motivation and self-determination in human behavior*. New York: Plenum Press.

Deci, E., & Ryan, R. (2009). Self Determination Theory: A consideration of human motivation universals. In P. J. Corr & G. Matthews (Eds.), *The Cambridge handbook of personality psychology* (pp. 441–456). New York, NY: Cambridge University Press.

Deci, E., Vallerand, R. J., Pelletier, L. G., & Ryan, R. M. (1991). Motivation and education: The self-determination perspective. *Educational Psychologist, 26*, 325–346.

English, R. (2015). Use your freedom of choice: Reasons for choosing homeschool in Australia. *Journal of Unschooling and Alternative Learning, 9*, 1–18.

Gardner, H. (1983). *Frames of mind: The theory of multiple intelligences*. New York: Basic Books.

Gardner, H. (1991). *The unschooled mind: How children think and how schools should teach*. New York: Basic Books.

Gardner, H. (1999). *Intelligence reframed: Multiple intelligences for the 21st century*. New York: Basic Books.

Gray, P. (2019, November 12). Kindergarten teachers speak out for children's happiness. *Freedom to Learn*. https://www.psychologytoday.com/us/blog/freedom-learn/201911/kindergarten-teachers-speak-out-children-s-hap piness.

Gray, P., & Riley, G. (2013). The challenges and benefits of unschooling according to 232 families who have chosen that route. *Journal of Unschooling and Alternative Learning, 7*(14), 1–27.

Gray, P., & Riley, G. (2015). Grown unschoolers' evaluation of their unschooling experiences: Report I on a survey of 75 unschooled adults. *Other Education, 4*(2), 8–32.

Halpert, J. (2018, June 5). Fostering connections between young and old. *The New York Times.* https://www.nytimes.com/2018/06/05/well/family/elderly-loneliness-aging-intergenerational-programs-.html.

Holt, J. (1964). *How children fail.* New York: Pitman Publishing Company.

Holt, J. (1967). *How children learn.* New York: Pitman Publishing Company.

Jacoby, J. (2010, March 6). Why one size fits all education doesn't work. *The Boston Globe.* http://archive.boston.com/bostonglobe/editorial_opinion/oped/articles/2010/03/06/why_one_size_fits_all_education_doesnt_work/.

Kirschner, D. H. (2008). *Producing unschoolers: Learning through living in a U.S. education movement* (Doctoral dissertation). University of Pennsylvania. ScholarlyCommons. http://repository.upenn.edu/dissertations/AAI3309459.

Kohn, A. (1993). *Punished by rewards: The trouble with gold stars, incentive plans, A's, praise, and other bribes.* Boston: Houghton Mifflin.

Kohn, A. (1999). *The schools our children deserve: Moving beyond traditional classrooms and tougher standards.* Boston: Houghton Mifflin.

Kohn, A. (2001, June 10). Why one size fits all education doesn't work. *The Boston Globe.* https://www.alfiekohn.org/article/one-size-fits-education-doesnt-work/.

Kohn, A. (2018, October 28). Rewards are still bad news (25 years later). *Alfiekohn.org.* https://www.alfiekohn.org/article/rewards-25-years-later/.

Lepper, M. R., Corpus, J., & Iyengar, S. (2005). Intrinsic and extrinsic motivational orientations in the classroom: Age differences and academic correlates. *Journal of Educational Psychology, 97*(2), 184–196.

Let Grow. (2019). https://letgrow.org/.

Levin-Guitterez, M. (2015). Motivation: Kept alive through unschooling. *Journal of Unschooling and Alternative Learning, 9*(17), 30–41.

Moss, E., & St. Laurent, D. (2001). Attachment at school age and academic performance. *Developmental Psychology, 37*(6), 863–874.

Neufield, G., & Mate, G. (2004). *Hold on to your kids: Why parents need to matter more than peers.* New York: Random House.

Nunez, J. L., & Leon, J. (2015). Autonomy support in the classroom: A review from Self-Determination Theory. *European Psychologist, 20*(4), 27–283.

Parkes, A. (2016, October 11). Rise of the home 'unschoolers'—Where children learn only what they want to. *The Guardian.* https://www.theguardian.com/education/2016/oct/11/unschool-children-monitor-home-schooling-education.

Piaget, J. (1952). *The origins of intelligence in children.* New York, NY: International Universities Press.

Piffero, E. (2020). *Io imparto da solo*. Florence, Italy: Terra Nuova.

Ratelle, C., Larose, S., Guay, F., & Senecal, C. (2005). Perceptions of parental involvement and support as predictors of college students' persistence in a science curriculum. *Journal of Family Psychology, 19*(2), 286–293.

Riley, G. (2018). A qualitative exploration of individuals who have identified as LGBTQ and who have homeschooled or unschooled. *Other Education, 7*(1), 3–17.

Ryan, R., & Deci, E. L. (2000). Self determination theory and the facilitation of intrinsic motivation, social development, and well being. *American Psychologist, 55*(1), 68–78.

Ryan, R., & Deci, E. L. (2017). *Self-Determination Theory: Basic psychological needs in motivation, development, and wellness*. New York: Guilford Press.

Ryan, R. M., & Powelson, C. L. (1991). Autonomy and relatedness as fundamental to motivation and education. *The Journal of Experimental Education, 60*(1), 49–66.

Sears, W. (2001). *The attachment parenting book: A commonsense guide to understanding and nurturing your baby*. Boston, MA: Little, Brown.

Sizer, B. B. (2012). *Unschooling 101*. http://www.pbs.org/parents/education/homeschooling/unschooling-101/.

Skenazy, L. (2008, April 1). Why I let my son ride the subway alone. *New York Sun*. https://www.nysun.com/news/why-i-let-my-9-year-old-ride-subway-alone.

Small, M. (1999). *Our babies, ourselves: How biology and culture shape the way we parent*. New York: Anchor Books.

Vallerand, R., Pelletier, L. G., & Koestner, R. (2008). Reflections on Self-Determination Theory. *Canadian Psychology, 49*(3), 252–262.

CHAPTER 4

Exploring the Growth of Homeschooling and Unschooling

Population

The number of families choosing to homeschool has grown exponentially in the past decade. Once a choice only made by religious conservatives or far-left hippies, homeschooling has grown to be one of a myriad of educational choices available to families (Gaither, 2018). From the year 1999 to 2012, the percentage of homeschooled students in the United States increased by 1.7%, with growth stabilizing between the years 2013 and 2016. Researchers now estimate that almost two million students in the United States are home educated, accounting for over 3% of the school-aged population (McQuiggan et al., 2017). This makes homeschooling a small but essential consideration for education policy experts, researchers, and stakeholders within the realm of education (Gaither, 2018). Although we have reliable data on the number of homeschoolers in the United States, estimating the percentage of those who unschool becomes more complicated. As Rolstad and Kesson (2013) express:

> …homeschooling families are still sometimes faced with hostility, and tend not to volunteer information about their educational status or activities. This is even more true of unschooling families, whose activities least resemble school, and are therefore least likely to volunteer their children for scrutiny by potentially prejudiced or judgmental observers. Unschooling families learn to navigate through the cracks and around the edges of what is considered to constitute 'appropriate' child experiences. (pp. 30–31)

G. Riley, *Unschooling*, Palgrave Studies in Alternative Education,
https://doi.org/10.1007/978-3-030-49292-2_4

Many families are hesitant to report that they unschool due to their particular state's homeschool regulations. For example, when examining the National Center for Education Statistics Data from 2016, 96.8% of respondents decided to skip the question that asked whether parents used a formal curriculum or informal learning method to homeschool their child (National Center for Education Statistics, 2016). However, unofficial estimates presume that around 10–20% of those who homeschool practice unschooling (Blanding, 2018), and that number seems to be growing every day.

Regulation

Homeschooling became legal in all fifty states in 1993 (Gaither, 2018). State homeschooling requirements vary from highly regulatory to less restrictive in nature. For example, in New York State, parents are required to send, at the beginning of the year, a Letter of Intent to homeschool and an Individual Home Instruction Plan, outlining all lessons and curriculum materials for each grade-based required subject. Attendance must be taken each day and attendance records must be submitted to the child's school district. Every three months, quarterly educational reports must be sent to the local district that include summaries and assessments in grade-based state-mandated subjects. An end of the year summary of educational activities completed is also required, along with proof that required achievement tests and/or end of the year assessments have been completed, depending on the grade the child is in (New York State Education Department, 2019). In neighboring New Jersey, a state with less restrictive homeschooling regulations, parents only need to maintain documentation that they are providing an equivalent education to that which is provided at their local public school, and simply need to show proof of that education in the event they are questioned by a state education department or government official (New Jersey State Education Department, 2019). The Home School Legal Defense Association (https://hslda.org/content/) provides state by state comparisons of homeschool regulations for those interested in comparing regulations. In terms of unschooling, it is easier to unschool legally in some states as compared to others, although unschooling can be done in many forms and in many ways.

Demographics

In the 1960s and 1970s the face of homeschooling mostly consisted of white religious or white liberal two-parent families (Gaither, 2018). However, that demographic has greatly changed as homeschooling has grown. Fifty-nine percent of homeschoolers are now non-Hispanic whites, and 8% of homeschoolers identify as black or African American. Three percent of homeschoolers identify as Asian. Interestingly, the number of homeschoolers who identify as Hispanic has jumped to 26% of all homeschoolers (McQuiggan et al., 2017). This is a particularly noteworthy increase, which Milter (2018) has attributed to three major reasons. First, Hispanic families may see the benefit of homeschooling in raising a bilingual child. A child who is homeschooled within a Hispanic family would be absorbed in both the Spanish language and the English language throughout their childhood and adolescence. Second, Hispanic families may be choosing to homeschool in higher numbers because of fear of racism, bullying, or racially charged incidents that have been happening in schools in greater numbers within the past four years. Finally, a larger number of Hispanics live in neighborhoods with struggling or low-funded schools, making homeschooling an attractive alternative.

The main reasons for homeschooling among black families include dissatisfaction with how their children are treated in schools and a culture of low expectation for black students that families observe within schools. There is also a strong feeling within the black community that there is an inability of schools to meet the needs of black students (Mazama and Lundy, 2013). This is evident when taking into consideration the disproportionate number of black students (especially black males) being referred for special education or behavior management interventions (Friend, 2013). Many families in Mazama and Lundy's study also mentioned the Euro-centric curriculum used in many schools that becomes a barrier for black children and adolescents. It is essential for all students to be able to see themselves within a curriculum, and in many cases, this is not the case for black children. Homeschooling or unschooling allows the parent or parents to create a more culturally relevant, equitable, and autonomous learning experience for their child.

The choice to homeschool is not an easy choice for black parents. According to Mazama "for African Americans there is a sense of betrayal when you leave public school in particular.... because the struggle to get into those schools was so harsh and so long" (Huseman, 2015). However, parents who have made the choice with courage and bravery are seeing vast benefits, as their children are thriving in a homeschooled environment (Huseman, 2015).

Gender and Education Distribution

In terms of gender distribution of homeschoolers, 52% of homeschoolers were reported as female, compared to 48% reported as male; and more homeschoolers (3.8% of all high schoolers) reported being in grades 9–12 as compared to 2.9% of all students reported as homeschooled in kindergarten through second grade. Some individuals are choosing to pull their children out of school at an older age, mostly because of long-standing bullying, school safety, or social issues. Other parents observe the academic successes of those who have homeschooled, and want to be part of the growing movement, especially as their child nears college application time. For some, homeschooling is seen as providing the unique educational experience that sets their teen apart from other applicants.

Of those doing homeschooling, 45% of homeschooling parents have a bachelor's or master's degree and 25% reported having a vocational degree or some college. Sixteen percent of homeschooling parents reported having a high school diploma only, and 15% of homeschooling parents reported never graduating high school (McQuiggan et al., 2017). Note that in most states, there is no minimum education credential needed for parents to homeschool their child. However, nine states require parents to, at minimum, have a high school diploma if they want to homeschool their child. Washington State has more stringent requirements. In Washington state, parents must either (1) be supervised by a certified person, (2) achieve a minimum number of college credits, (3) take a course in home-based instruction, or (4) be deemed as "qualified" by their local school board to homeschool (Home School Legal Defense Association, 2020).

Regarding economic status, in 2016, there was a spike in the percentage of homeschooled children reported as poor. In 2012, 11% of homeschooled children reported being poor, as compared to 21% in 2016 (McQuiggan et al., 2017). This increase in homeschooled students identified as poor may be attributed to families choosing homeschooling who live in areas where school districts are lower funded and more scarcely staffed. It may also be attributed to the increase in more single parents who are choosing to homeschool. In addition, it has been observed that many parents are giving up their primary career or an additional income source in order to homeschool their child (Fields-Smith and Kisura, 2013), making financial sacrifices themselves in order to prioritize their child's educational and personal advancement.

In terms of unschooling demographics, the assumption is that data is similar to those who identify as homeschoolers. However, wide-spanning quantitative demographic and informational data on unschoolers has not yet been collected. Research on unschooling is currently in its infancy, and all research thus far focusing on unschoolers has been qualitative. Also, as stated previously, unschoolers tend to be difficult to quantify, and understandably tend to distrust formal external examination and study. The Gray and Riley (2013) study below may create only a small snapshot of what unschooling really looks like, but does give us some relevant data.

In Gray and Riley's study of 232 unschooling families, 221 (95.2%) of those who responded were mothers, 9 were fathers, and 2 were unschooled young adults writing about their family of origin. Two hundred and ten (90.5%) of the respondents identified themselves as married and/or living with a significant other. Regarding the number of children in the family, 21.6% had one child, 44.8% had two children, and 33.6% had more than three children. Roughly half the respondents identified as stay-at-home mothers, some of whom also pursued part-time work. Fathers were identified as working full-time. The responses concerning employment of both mothers and fathers created the assumption that these families represented a wide range in terms of socioeconomic status. Many respondents identified themselves as being professionals, others defined themselves as self-employed, while still others defined themselves as being blue-collar workers. As stated previously, the results of this study may not adequately capture the full picture of what the unschooling population may look like demographically, but it does give us some important information to consider.

Motivations for Homeschooling and Unschooling

While religious motivation was previously the number one reason why parents decided to homeschool their children, it is not anymore. According to data from the National Center for Education Statistics, the top three stated motivations for homeschooling included (1) concern regarding the child's school environment (34%), (2) dissatisfaction with academic instruction at school (17%), and (3) a desire to provide religious education (16%). Other reasons parents saw as important in their decision to homeschool were concerns regarding the environment of their neighborhood schools (school safety, drug/alcohol usage, or negative peer pressure), a desire to provide moral or character-based instruction, and dissatisfaction with current academic instruction. Approximately 12% of the population chose homeschooling because of their children's special needs, including physical or mental health needs (McQuiggan et al., 2017). Under federal law, local school districts are required to provide free evaluation to students who are homeschooled. However, the ability to get services or receive an Individualized Education Plan (IEP) for a homeschooled student with special needs varies from state to state (Friend, 2013). Michaud (2019) discusses her experience in homeschooling, and then unschooling a child with Fetal Alcohol Syndrome, Attention Deficit Hyperactivity Disorder, and a Learning Disability in her article "Healing Through Unschooling". In it, she states that when unschooling "I was no longer riddled with anxiety and the need to control him and started genuinely enjoying his company....Our relationship was stronger and more loving. And he started learning to do many things on his own (including reading without teaching)".

Evidence has also appeared further discussing an increase in the number of Muslim and black families choosing to homeschool. Within the Islamic community, Muslim families are sometimes hesitant to send their children to public schools, where teaching can sometimes run contrary to Muslim belief and culture. Also, some Muslim students may experience prejudice within the classroom because of differences in appearance, dress, or cultural traditions. Homeschooling has appeared as a relevant, viable option for these families (Jackson, 2012). As mentioned previously, within the black community there has been a rise in the number of parents intentionally seeking alternatives to public schools. Field-Smith and Williams (2009) did a mixed methods study on twenty-four black parents who chose to homeschool, and found that "Black families perceived that institutional norms and structures within schools created destructive, rather than supportive learning environments" (p. 276). This included curriculum, classroom, and behavior management structures. Mazama and Lundy studied seventy-four black homeschooling parents and found that reasons for homeschooling included concerns regarding the quality of education their child was receiving, wanting to strengthen familial and community bonding, and a desire on the part of the parents to be able to teach their children utilizing curriculum that positively reflects African American culture (2013). Akilah Richards, podcaster, author, and founding board member of the Alliance for Self Directed Education, reiterates this view, stating "We cannot keep using tools of oppression and expect to raise free people" (2019b).

Homeschooling, Unschooling, and Those Who Identify as LGBTQ

In 2016, the author of this book completed the first qualitative study of individuals who identified as Lesbian, Gay, Bisexual, Transgender, or Queer/Questioning who have homeschooled or unschooled. Although not much is known regarding actual percentages of LGBTQ students who are homeschooled or unschooled, it is informally assumed that around 5–10% of homeschoolers identify as LGBTQ, with some estimates maintaining that the percentage may be closer to 20% (Riley, 2018). Overall, individuals in the study who were homeschooled or unschooled and identified as LGBTQ reported positive experiences. Many felt that the freedom and autonomy inherently present in many homeschooled and unschooled environments made it easier to explore one's gender identification and sexual preference openly and without judgment. Others stated that because they were homeschooled or unschooled, they got to escape heteronormative school culture and also got a chance to embrace who they were in a less pressured way. As examples, one person shared:

> I think that the biggest benefit of being homeschooled and bisexual was the strength it gave me to be myself. As a homeschooler, I always knew I was different; not going to school made me grow up outside of the norm. I absolutely loved being homeschooled, and because I loved it so much, this helped me realize that being different could be a wonderful thing. So, when I started figuring out my sexuality and realized just how that would go over with my peers, my homeschooling experience helped combat the negativity. I already had experience being different, and it wasn't inherently a bad thing to be different from other people. (Riley, 2018, p. 10)

Another expressed:

> I think homeschooling and unschooling first and foremost allowed me to question social norms in general. Not having to do the thing that is

> supposed to completely define teenagerhood—go to school—opened up the possibility of being able to question everything else I was supposed to do. I had always leaned towards trusting my own understanding and knowledge over any that was outright handed to me, and generally questioned anything that didn't make sense, but homeschooling gave me even greater permission to do that. I had the opportunity to come to my own conclusions about the world, and gender and sexuality were part of that. The more specific stuff came later, in college, when I started taking classes in gender history. I'm not sure if I would have started identifying as trans had that not happened....Reading texts on the history of sexuality and gender theory once again allowed me to question the social norms that I was supposed to adhere to. If gender categories had been invented anyway, there was no need for me to define myself according to them; I could make up a new way of being. I can't say for sure if that was related to homeschooling, but I wouldn't be surprised if that ability to rapidly throw out social rules that didn't make sense to me was in some way rooted in my history of dropping out of middle school to educate myself. (Riley, 2018, p. 12)

More research must be done within this area, as many participants in this study expressed that the home and/or unschooling environment gave them not only a sense of freedom and discovery, but also a sense of safety and comfort during particularly sensitive and challenging times.

Other Notable Population Increases

There has also been anecdotal data stating that homeschooling is increasing in popularity among military families that frequently move (Prothero, 2018), as well as among families who have chosen not to vaccinate their children. The increase in non-vaccinated students registering to home educate was seen especially between 2016 and 2020 within the states of California and New York. Both states have implemented strict immunization laws, requiring all students to be updated on their vaccines if they choose to attend public or private schools. Parents who oppose compulsory vaccinations are now choosing homeschooling in greater numbers, finding comfort not only in their freedom of medical choice, but also in freedom of educational choice. Homeschooling and unschooling cooperatives are also seeing increases in numbers of attendees because of changes in vaccine laws (Bellafante, 2019; Karlamangla, 2019).

Mash Ups: Homeschooling, Unschooling, and School

Those who study demographics of homeschoolers believe there may be some variety in government data presented on homeschooling. For example, some homeschoolers may not register with their state or district, fearful of government infringement. Other homeschoolers who are enrolled part time in public schools, or within online charter schools, registered free schools, or learning centers may be double-counted or not counted at all as homeschoolers (Gaither, 2018). Some homeschoolers may be sixteen years of age and older, and already enrolled and counted as community college or college students. Even the National Center for Education Statistics admits their data on homeschoolers is incomplete, as their non response rate is higher for their homeschooled survey as compared to other surveys (Silva, 2018).

Homeschoolers, Unschoolers, and Life Success

A common worry among parents, homeschoolers, and the public is "how do homeschoolers get into college?" However, in this arena, homeschoolers seem to be doing just fine. Many homeschoolers enroll in community college classes at age 16, getting both an early start on college and an official college transcript to illustrate their knowledge within a particular subject. Other high school aged homeschoolers use the College Level Examination Program, or CLEP tests (https://clep.collegeboard.org/) to gain college credit for learning they have done at home (Silva, 2018). Also, an increased number of homeschoolers seem to be taking more Advanced Placement tests as well as more formal aptitude tests like the ACT (College Board, 2019; Gaither, 2018). Surveys of adults who have been homeschooled conclude that homeschooling leads to more positive life outcomes, including increased college attendance, increased college GPA's, greater overall life satisfaction, and higher levels of personal competence and autonomy as compared to traditionally schooled peers (Ray, 2003; Riley, 2015). Homeschooled students are also more likely to be civically engaged in their communities (Ray, 2003) due to the increased amount of time spent in those communities, instead of being limited by the microcosm of school. As stated by Gaither, "in 1986, 90% of the nations' colleges and universities had no explicit homeschooling admissions policy. By 2004, over 75% did, and the vast majority of admissions officers surveyed then, and again in 2013, reported very positive feelings about homeschooled applicants" (2018, p. 273).

Although homeschooling is quickly joining the ranks of private schools and charter schools as an acceptable alternative to public education, literature on young adult outcomes of unschooling is scarce. In a world that loves data and numbers, many wonder how those who are unschooled compare in overall readiness to their schooled or homeschooled peers. To date, there have been only two peer-reviewed academic studies on life outcomes of those who have been unschooled (Gray and Riley, 2015; Riley and Gray, 2015). There have, however, been several instances of young adult unschoolers sharing their stories within mainstream books, media, and websites (Boles, 2020; Kowalke, 2001; Patterson, 2015; Stuart, 2020). In terms of unschooling data and college, Riley and Gray did a qualitative study of 75 grown unschoolers in 2015. Within that study, they learned that 83% had gone on to some form of higher education after unschooling. Of that 83%, 44% had either completed a bachelor's degree or were enrolled in a bachelor's degree program. Unschoolers were similar to homeschoolers in their methods of getting into college, including using community college transcripts as an entry way to gaining admissions, taking a high school equivalency exam, or utilizing a portfolio or interview to start the process of college admissions. A majority of unschooled students within the Riley and Gray study felt that unschooling gave them an upper hand in college, as the intrinsic motivation and self-direction they utilized while unschooling assisted them in succeeding within the realm of higher education (2015).

Unschooling Data and Research

As Rolstad and Kesson (2013) state, "definitions of unschooling vary widely, and the philosophies and activities of unschooling also vary tremendously. Further complicating large scale research efforts, unschooling families can also be difficult to locate and study" (p. 30). Although some research has been conducted on unschooling families and unschooled young adult outcomes (Gray and Riley, 2013; Gray and Riley, 2015; Riley and Gray, 2015), both qualitative and quantitative research on unschooling must be greatly expanded in the future.

There are organizations, nonprofits, and journals that support research on homeschooling, unschooling, and other forms of alternative education that deserve recognition. The Alternative Education Resource Organization (AERO) is one such nonprofit. Founded in 1989 by Jerry Mintz, AERO has promoted books and hosted yearly conferences on homeschooling, unschooling, and alternative learning environments. AERO has provided many academics and researchers time and space, in person, through virtual online conferences, and in print, to discuss their research findings and share them with others.

Dr. Carlo Ricci, a professor at Nipissing University in Canada, created *The Journal of Unschooling and Alternative Learning* in 2008. This journal provides scholars with a peer-reviewed outlet to submit research within the realm of homeschooling, unschooling, and alternative learning. The journal's importance must be highlighted, as some major traditional education journals reject or do not understand the premise of unschooling, and therefore tend to reject research relating to it. Dr. Helen Lees, founder and editor of the journal *Other Education: The Journal of Educational Alternatives* must also be mentioned. *Other Education* is another major peer-reviewed journal that offers scholars in the fields of homeschooling, unschooling, and alternative or democratic education a place to submit academic research for consideration.

Knowing that scholars and academics need a place to discuss research ideas prior to submitting their work to peer-reviewed journals, the Alliance for Self-Directed Education has recently started a research group for those interested and involved in research focusing on all forms of self-directed learning. This research group has been invaluable as a circle for discussing, sharing, and promoting academic research related to alternative learning environments. The group has a private Facebook page and hosts monthly online meetings. All researchers, academics, and graduate students involved in research on unschooling, homeschooling, or self-directed learning are invited to participate.

As the unschooling movement grows, research needs to grow with it. Thanks to pioneers such as Jerry Mintz, Carlo Ricci, Helen Lees, and Peter Gray, there are spaces where research related to unschooling and alternative learning can be formulated, discussed, and published. These spaces need to be promoted—as it is research that gives legitimacy to the field of unschooling. The hope is that as unschooling increases in popularity, more individuals and families within the movement will find the time and interest to become an active part of scientific studies on unschooling, and share their experiences with those collecting academic and census-based data on unschooling. Sharing stories, experiences, and data will help propel the movement forward as a recognized and accepted educational choice for families across the United States and all over the world.

References

Alliance for Self Directed Education. (2019). https://www.self-directed.org/.

Alternative Education Resource Organization. (2019). https://www.educationrevolution.org.

Bellafante, G. (2019, September 13). How far would you go to avoid vaccinating your child? *The New York Times*. https://www.nytimes.com/2019/09/13/nyregion/vaccination-homeschooling-new-york-city.html.

Blanding, M. (2018, October 2). Twenty percent of home schooled kids are getting 'unschooled'. What's that? *The Boston Globe*. https://www.bostonglobe.com/magazine/2018/10/02/home-schoolers-turn-boston-area-new-unschooling-centers/j4TB7K54hm7V7ri0yDPTlM/story.html.

Boles, B. (2020). *Grown Unschoolers*. https://grownunschoolers.com/about/.

College Board. (2019). *AP Central: Student datafile*. https://apcentral.collegeboard.org/scores/available-reports/student-datafile.

Fields-Smith, C., & Kisura, M. W. (2013). Resisting the status quo: The narratives of black homeschoolers in metro Atlanta and metro DC. *Peabody Journal of Education, 88*, 265–283.

Fields-Smith, C., & Williams, M. R. (2009). Sacrifices, challenges and empowerment: Black parents' decisions to home school. *Urban Review, 41*, 369–389.

Friend, M. (2013). *Special education: Contemporary perspectives for school professionals*. New York: Pearson Education.

Gaither, M. (2018). *Homeschool: An American history*. New York: Palgrave Macmillan.

Gray, P., & Riley, G. (2013). The challenges and benefits of unschooling according to 232 families who have chosen that route. *Journal of Unschooling and Alternative Learning, 7*, 1–27.

Gray, P. & Riley, G. (2015). Grown unschoolers' evaluations of their unschooling experience: Report I on a survey of 75 unschooled adults. Other Education, Volume 4, Issue 2, 8-32.

Home School Legal Defense Association (HSDLA). (2020). https://hslda.org/content/.

Huseman, J. (2015, February 17). The rise of the African American homeschoolers. *The Atlantic*. https://www.theatlantic.com/education/archive/2015/02/the-rise-of-homeschooling-among-black-families/385543/.

Jackson, D. (2012, February 21). Muslim families turn to home schooling. *The Washington Times*. https://www.washingtontimes.com/news/2012/feb/21/muslim-families-turn-to-home-schooling/.

Journal of Unschooling and Alternative Learning (*JUAL*). (2019). https://jual.nipissingu.ca/.

Karlamangla, S. (2019, July 23). Parents who won't vaccinate their kids turning to homeschooling in California. *The Los Angeles Times*. https://www.latimes.com/california/story/2019-07-22/california-homeschool-strict-vaccination-laws.

Kowalke, P. (2001). *Grown Without Schooling*. https://www.peterkowalke.com/.

Mazama, A., & Lundy, G. (2013). African American homeschooling and the question of curricular cultural relevance. *The Journal of Negro Education, 82*(2), 123–138.

McQuiggan, M., Megra, M., & Grady, S. (2017). *Parent and family involvement in education: Results from the National Household Education Surveys Program of 2016*. Washington, DC: National Center for Education Statistics.

Michaud, D. (2019). Healing through unschooling. *Journal of Unschooling and Alternative Learning, 26,* 1–13.

Miltner, O. (2018, March 22). *The new face of U.S. homeschooling is Hispanic*. https://www.ozy.com/fast-forward/the-new-face-of-u-s-homeschooling-is-hispanic/85278/.

National Center for Education Statistics. (2016). *Data on home education*. https://nces.ed.gov/nhes/data/2016/cbook_pfi_pu.pdf.

New Jersey State Education Department. (2019). *Homeschooling*. https://www.state.nj.us/education/students/safety/edservices/hs/.

New York State Education Department. (2019). *Part 100 regulations: Home instruction*. http://www.p12.nysed.gov/part100/pages/10010.html.

Other Education: The Journal of Educational Alternatives. (2019). https://www.othereducation.org/index.php/OE/issue/view/15.

Patterson, S. W. (2015). *Homeschooled teens: 75 young people speak about their lives without school*. Wimberley, TX: Second Tier Publishing.

Prothero, A. (2018, January 10). Homeschooling: Requirements, research and who does it. *Education Week*. https://www.edweek.org/ew/issues/home-schooling/index.html.

Ray, B. (2003). Homeschooling Grows Up. *Home School Legal Defense Association*. https://www.hslda.org/research/ray2003/HomeschoolingGrowsUp.pdf.

Richards, A. (2019a, December 27). Personal Communication.

Richards, A. (2019b). *Raising free people*. https://www.raisingfreepeople.com/about/.

Riley, G. (2015). Differences in levels of competence, autonomy, and relatedness between home educated and traditionally educated young adults. *International Social Science Review, 2,* 1–27.

Riley, G. (2018). A qualitative exploration of the experiences of individuals who have identified as LGBTQ and who have homeschooled or unschooled. *Other Education, 7*(1), 3–17.

Riley, G., & Gray, P. (2015). Grown unschoolers' experiences with higher education and employment: Report II on a survey of 75 unschooled adults. *Other Education, 4*(2), 33–53.

Rolstad, K., & Kesson, K. (2013). Unschooling, then and now. *Journal of Unschooling and Alternative Learning, 7*, 30–49.

Silva, E. (2018, September 21). The state of homeschooling in America. *Pacific Standard.* https://psmag.com/education/the-state-of-homeschooling-in-america.

Stuart, J. (Director) (2020). *Self taught: Life stories for self-directed learners* [Film]. https://www.selftaughtmovie.com/.

CHAPTER 5

The Spectrum of Unschooling

Individuals learn through exploration and interaction with their environment. For most children in school, this means classroom interaction with certified teachers and same-aged peers. This also means required textbooks, assignments, and assessments, selected for the child as part of a pre-planned curriculum (Gray and Riley, 2013). Curriculum is either required by the state, or purchased by the district as part of an agreed-upon curriculum initiative. Curriculum should be age appropriate, culturally relevant, and differentiated for all learners, but many times, it is not. Curriculum and state-based standards are created for groups of same-aged individuals on a similar trajectory of social, emotional, and intellectual growth. Basically, seventh-grade curriculum and standards are created for the "average" twelve-year-old, without taking into consideration individual interests, strengths, and talents. Also, most curriculum is classroom-based, meaning a majority of work planned within the curriculum is created to be completed seated on chairs at a desk. If the main goal of school is to prepare students for the "real world," when does interaction with that world happen? What if a child's classroom was actually the "real world," as it is in unschooling?

It is difficult to define unschooling formally, as the practice is, by nature, informal (Gray and Riley, 2013). It was John Holt who coined the term unschooling in the 70s as a play on the popular 7 Up "Un-cola" advertisement in that time, when 7 Up was being marketed as something new and different as compared to traditional sodas like Coca-Cola or

G. Riley, *Unschooling*, Palgrave Studies in Alternative Education,
https://doi.org/10.1007/978-3-030-49292-2_5

Pepsi-Cola (Dodd, 2019). Thus, he came up with the term unschooled: a new and different way of schooling. Sandra Dodd, an unschooling pioneer who unschooled her own children in the 80s through 2000s, has also defined it as "creating and maintaining an environment in which natural learning can flourish" (2019). Many current unschoolers take issue with the term "unschooling," as to them, it sounds like children engaged in unschooling are not learning. Instead, they prefer the terms self directed education, autonomous education, or willed education (Alliance for Self-Directed Education, 2020; Ricci, 2012).

In 2008, Donna Kirschner published a dissertation focused on examining the countercultural unschooling movement. She reviewed topics such as unschooling and its relationship to attachment parenting, parental use of time and space, the relationship of unschooling families to their communities, and how unschooling was legitimatized to the outside world by use of portfolio and narrative. Within her ethnographic dissertation, she explained that in the unschooling families she studied, a major goal was to facilitate their child's intrinsic motivation. They also focused on self-understanding, or having their children really know themselves deeply as humans. Because of this internal and intrinsic focus, traditional forms of assessment and evaluation don't seem to make sense to unschoolers and are seen as "disruptive to learning" (2008, p. 44). Qualitative, organic self-assessment comes naturally to unschoolers.

In their large-scale study of unschooling families, Gray and Riley (2013) attempted to define unschooling in depth for the purposes of their research based on previous definitions and explanations. They created this definition:

> Unschoolers do not send their children to school, and they do not do at home the kinds of things that are done in school. More specifically, they do not establish a curriculum for their children, they do not require their children to do particular assignments for the purpose of education, and they do not test their children to measure progress. Instead, they allow their children freedom to pursue their own interests and to learn, in their own ways, what they need to know to follow those interests. They also, in various ways, provide an environmental context and environmental support for their child's learning. Life and learning do not occur in a vacuum, they occur in the context of a cultural environment, and unschooling parents help define and bring the child into contact with that environment. (p. 7)

In doing their research, Gray and Riley (2013) discovered that parents tended to categorize their form of unschooling based on how much freedom and autonomy they gave their children. This categorization is relatively new, and was not a conversation that unschoolers in the 60s through 90s engaged in. However, an increase in the popularity of unschooling has generated specific discussions of unschooling philosophy, and thus, the need for more defined categories (Dodd, 2019). For some unschoolers, these defined categories seem limiting and exclusionary. For others, having defined categories has been helpful in strengthening and communicating one's personal philosophy of learning. For example, one parent in Gray and Riley's study shared:

> I know many advocates of unschooling are particular with definitions. I am not. For many years I did not consider myself an unschooler, nor did I want to be included in the narrow singular definition that was available at the time. I am a person that recoils with the thought of being classified or labelled. As more people become familiar with the aspect of homeschool, I feel a need to self-identify somewhat with the less rigid, free-flowing, and interest-led group of individuals that identify themselves as unschoolers. (2013)

In the case above, the parent sees a distinct difference between the terms homeschooling and unschooling. However, unschoolers have further defined themselves, needing more salient terminology for the different types of learning and environments they facilitate. Three main classifications of unschooling most frequently used are Relaxed Homeschooling, Unschooling, and Radical Unschooling.

Relaxed Homeschooling

As stated previously, people who identify themselves as unschoolers vary in their educational practices and beliefs (Gray and Riley, 2013). Some people who define themselves as unschoolers must follow a curriculum based on their particular state's regulations. Others feel more comfortable following a curriculum to guide their children's learning or their school-based year. The curriculum used is generally not applied on a day by day basis, but serves to provide some structure and direction to learning. The curriculum may also be used to provide a framework for subject-specific learning on state-required quarterly reports or end of the year summaries. Families within the relaxed homeschooling category either have some academic standards and goals for their children, or feel that it is their responsibility as parents to provide some formal academic-based structures for their children. Children or teens within this category are encouraged to explore subjects, ideas, and hobbies that are of particular interest to them, and can spend as much time as they would like on their own self-determined learnings or skills.

Ree Drummond, a blogger and television personality also known as "The Pioneer Woman," has practiced relaxed homeschooling for most of her children's lives. As she explained in a 2007 blog post:

> When I first started out, the fear and uncertainty I felt about homeschooling caused me to go a little berserk. In preparation for that first year, I created an intricate color-coded chart that accounted for each and every thirty-minute time slot from 6 am to 4 pm. I followed my psychotic color-coded schedule to a T…for four days. Then I gave up….I've settled comfortably into this life—this life of a relaxed homeschooler. Now, I do have specific, quality materials I use, but I've come a long way from the "thirty-minute goal" approach with which I began…My goals are yearly these days. I know what grade my kids are in, what materials they'll need to attain a certain level of knowledge by the end of the year, and I jump in. Some days, I'm pleased with the amount of work we get done. Other days, we never look at a book because the kids are working cattle or I decide I can't be bothered with Advanced Physics…

Relaxed homeschooling is not school at home. Instead, relaxed homeschooling allows for the child or teen to take control of their own learning, with some focused facilitation organized by the parent. This may look like a once per academic quarter review of things learned, or a yearly informal evaluation of progress made toward individual goals. It also may look like a child or teen spending one or two hours per day on assigned work, with the rest of the day free for autonomous exploration or self-chosen activities. One parent in Gray and Riley's (2013) study explained how relaxed homeschooling looked in their home, stating "We do have a curriculum, but it's a guide for us, not for them. We provide opportunities for them to try new things that we think are developmentally appropriate. But if they are not interested, that is fine." Another parent expressed that it was their job to be a guiding force in their children's learning and development. As she shared:

> In my opinion, my responsibilities as a parent for my children's education are absolute. It is my sole responsibility to prepare them for a fulfilling life (according to their own definition, not mine or society's)....Having stated that, I think there is not a chance knowledge will be retained if it is forced upon the child. It is my role to enhance my children's lives with as many opportunities and learning moments as indicated or possible. I am their first and only advocate until they learn to advocate for themselves. I need to recognize their interests and embellish upon different learning techniques that widen their sphere of influence and understanding of the world they live in because those resources are available to me primarily in our culture. As a parent, I am their role model, mentor, advisor, and learning facilitator. (2013)

Although some structured academic work may be involved, relaxed homeschooling allows one's unique relationships with their children to be front and center, creating an individualized arena for learning and growing. Academic work may be introduced, but it is not the main focus of the day. In an environment of relaxed homeschooling, the parent is the facilitator, but not director, of the child's learning.

Unschooling

In the first issue of *Growing Without Schooling*, John Holt stated, "children want to learn about the world, are good at it, and can be trusted to do it without much adult coercion or interference" (1977, p. 1). Those who unschool know this, and typically allow their children freedom with regards to how they spend their days. Instead of following a set curriculum, unschooling parents may ask "What do you want to learn today? How do you want to set this up?" (Hanes, 2016). Ben Hewitt, an author and homeschooling dad, explains "Perhaps the best way to explain it is that all unschooling is homeschooling, but not all homeschooling is unschooling. While most homeschooled children follow a structured curriculum, unschoolers like have almost total autonomy over their days" (2014). One parent describes unschooling in this way:

> For us, unschooling is self-directed, interest driven, freedom-based learning all the time. We do not use curriculum, nor do we have certain days or hours when we schedule learning. We are learning as we live. We view learning as a natural part of humanity, and we believe that learning is naturally joyful and desirable. We value a spirit of wonder, play, and meaningful

> connection with others. We seek to experience education as a meaningful, experiential, explorative, joyful, passionate life. We see the parents' role as facilitating a peaceful, happy, interesting environment; answering or helping find answers to questions when asked...and providing access to resources, people, and opportunities, especially as desired by our children. (Gray and Riley, 2013)

As Mary Griffith, author of *The Unschooling Handbook*, states "the first requirement of unschooling is that children spend the bulk of their time in places where learning and exploration are possible and welcome" (1998, p. 6). This place can be their home, their backyard, their neighborhood, the local library, a museum, or even a relative or friend's home. Unschooling parents will answer questions and facilitate the finding of resources and materials that support a child or teen's interests. Being an unschooling parent is almost like being a librarian. The individual says, "I'm interested in this particular topic" and the unschooling parent will find ways to support that interest. After a while, the unschooled child or teen will learn how to find resources themselves, without adult assistance. The ability to effectively find resources is why many individuals who have encountered unschooled children or teens note that an unschoolers' greatest strength is that they instinctively know how to learn, or how to find information on topics or skills they want to learn. Unschoolers have been practicing the skill of learning how to learn all of their lives.

Radical Unschooling

Radical unschooling is a specific form of unschooling where a child has full and complete autonomy, both over their days and over their individual schedule. Within the Gray and Riley (2013) study, radical unschooling was described as an environment where parents "did not deliberately attempt to motivate, guide, direct, or monitor their child's learning; any involvement in that learning was at the child's request" (p. 7). Olsen (2020) suggests that radical unschooling is not just about learning. Radical unschooling takes the philosophy of unschooling and extends it to tasks of daily living. For example, in some families who engage in radical unschooling, children and teens have full autonomy over when they eat, sleep, watch television, play video games and engage in household tasks. Rather than rules, families live and learn guided by familial principals or basic ethics. Olsen reminds people that radical unschooling is not "unparenting." Instead, it is a mindful and intentional way of collaborating with one's children (2020). A radical unschooling parent in Gray and Riley's (2013) study describes their role as "that of a supporter. I follow my kid's interests. He has time and space to learn in the way he wants to learn. We don't really follow rules or guidelines. We discuss everything together."

It is radical unschooling that has received the most critical press in recent years (ABC News-Nightline, 2010; Dr. Phil Show, 2011; Wife Swap, 2013a). For instance, radical unschooler Dayna Martin has, several times, allowed her and her family to be filmed going about their days, living and learning with no school, curriculum, bedtime, or rules. Unschoolers have appreciated the press and the Martin family's openness in allowing cameras into their home. However, viewers with more traditional backgrounds have candidly stated concerns with the lack of traditional discipline and structure they see in the Martin home. During a *Dr. Phil* episode where the Martin's were featured, Dr. Phil McGraw questioned: "Do you worry that by not providing structure and goals and some kind of timeline, so they can experience themselves master some things, meet some goals…that they're not going to be ready to compete in the outside world?". Dayna replied, "We're in the real world every day. It's kids in school that are in a building all day, away from the real world" (2011). Martin describes radical unschooling as joyful, peaceful parenting. She reports that her children are already entrepreneurs, making money off pursuing interests and passions. In terms of parenting, Martin states that when one of her children does something wrong, they talk about it. They try to find win-win solutions, and believe that respect and kindness are the most important qualities a family can feel toward each other (Martin, 2013b)

Those who provide an environment that supports radical unschooling instinctively understand that in order to make healthy decisions, children and teens must practice decision-making, every day, and in every aspect of their lives. Radical unschoolers see health and safety, and the health and safety of others, as most important and non-negotiable. Everything else is secondary and can be learned and absorbed through interaction with life and with people. Radical unschoolers have full agency over their life and how they spend their days.

Although the spectrum of unschooling is well known to unschooling parents and those within the movement, researchers have not formally studied different types of unschoolers using a quantitative methodology. The one source of data we do have is the results of the Gray and Riley study of 232 unschooling families. Within that qualitative study, researchers asked, "Please describe briefly how your family defines unschooling. What if any responsibility do you, as parent(s), assume for your child's education?" (2013, p. 7). Responses were coded based on descriptions respondents gave. Based on that coding, 43.5% of respondents used language that would define themselves as radical unschoolers, 41.4% responded in a way that implied that they unschooled; and 15.1% participants responded in a way that implied they relaxed homeschooled.

Developing an Acceptance of Unschooling

In the 1970s, most homeschooling involved doing school at home, complete with desks, chairs, and a standardized curriculum. In many states, home learning was still illegal, so parents homeschooled in hiding, fearful of government punishment (and having their children taken away). The court case Wisconsin vs. Yoder (1972) changed things significantly. In Wisconsin vs. Yoder, the United States Supreme Court ruled that Amish children could not be forced to go to school past 8th grade, citing a citizen's fundamental right to freedom of religion. Although this specific court case focused on the Amish and their beliefs, it was Chief Justice Warren Burger's opinion that questioned the overall rationale of compulsory schooling. His questioning became a strong argument for allowing children and adolescents the right to be educated outside of public or private school. Justice William O. Douglas also argued that students, not only parents, should also be able to express if they want to continue with schooling (1972).

This ruling opened up the conversation about compulsory schooling, a conversation John Holt was already a part of. The nation began questioning the standardization of education, and how much freedom parents could and should have in making educational decisions for their child. The topic of education became a national conversation. Schools weren't working for many students, and school reform was made a governmental agenda item. The focus shifted not to more regulation, per se, but toward how to create optimal situations for school-aged children. As Professor Michael Katz expressed in 1976:

> Having expected miracles from increased schooling, the public has no choice but to live with the limitations of education. If a gap exists between the ideal of universal education and the realities of compulsory schooling, it is no surprise. Rather, concern should focus on how to narrow this gap. Finally, in seeking to free rather than imprison the child, promote growth rather than stunt it, and foster individual welfare rather than harm it, not only the quality of schools but also the quality of the society in which young people are growing up must be improved. (p. 35)

Through the promotion of unschooling as a viable educational option, John Holt was attempting to make a dent in increasing the quality of society for both children and adults alike. Schools weren't going to be easily fixed, so parents needed to know that they had the ability to bring their children home and guide their education in a way that made sense to them. Communities could assist by embracing unschoolers, and individuals with specific talents and occupational strengths could be seen as skill models for children. Holt proposed that intensive amounts of teaching were interfering with students actually learning, driving him to reassure parents that a child could indeed direct their own educational path (1977).

Many embraced the call. For some, unschooling was seen as a natural approach to learning, and was welcomed as a natural next step after breastfeeding and babywearing. To others, unschooling was discovered after a period of curriculum-based homeschooling (Griffith, 1998). Early unschoolers had the support of Holt and *Growing Without Schooling*, even though they sometimes faced challenges that complicated the ability to allow their child's intrinsic motivation to direct learning. Although unschooling was in many cases difficult to legally practice, organizations such as the Homeschool Legal Defense Association (HSLDA, 2020), founded in 1983, assisted parents in knowing their rights, and supported parents when they were questioned by authorities. The National Home Education Research Institute (NHERI), founded in 1990 by Dr. Brian Ray, also gave support through research and advocacy when parents felt questioned or persecuted.

Unschooling in the 1990s was still difficult, as homeschooling had just become legal in all 50 states in 1993, and not many people admitted to unschooling, as it was still seen as different and risky. This made socializing with others and gaining outside support challenging. However, the growing popularity of the internet made things a bit easier, as there were many AOL message boards focused on homeschoolers, and then unschoolers who were "coming out," looking for a place to discuss and share experiences (Dodd, 2019). By the mid-nineties, many parents felt comfortable calling themselves unschoolers, but only within open, accepting social circles or via specific internet listservs and message boards.

By contrast, a significantly different time and space for unschoolers has emerged in the twenty-first century. Isolation has been resolved by an increased unschooling population, the rising influence of social media, and a plethora of blogs, websites, and other online sources focusing on unschooling. Prior to the 2000s, there was no real spectrum of unschooling. Those unschooling were just doing it, quietly, without much discussion about what type of unschooling they ascribed to. However, as unschooling grew, and social media became a primary forum for discussions around unschooling, differences within groups became more apparent, and it was not only based on how much curriculum families did or did not use. At first, the differences centered around parenting style, as unschooling parents began to discuss and debate how to best define their respective classification. To be a radical unschooler, does one have to be a permissive parent? If you let your child play video games all day, but gave your children a specific bedtime, could you still be considered a radical unschooler? Does one have to practice attachment parenting to unschool? Then, the focus centered on academic requirements: What if an individual just used curriculum because their state required it? Could a person still be considered an unschooler, or were they automatically placed in the relaxed homeschooling category?

As vaccination laws became more stringent within schools, parents opposed to vaccination became associated with the movement, creating a connection between "anti vaxxers" and unschooling (McBroom, 2012). Recently, those within the libertarian movement have been vocal about a link between their political views and unschooling (McDonald, 2019), creating intense discussion within the unschooling community regarding whether politics and unschooling should ever go together. There are already many stereotypes attached to unschoolers, and the fear is that these recently developed associations may create even more (McBroom, 2012).

Mainstream Criticisms of Unschooling

Unschooling has always been ripe with stereotypes and criticisms, as there is a lack of understanding from the general public regarding what unschooling is all about. Houseman (2011) did a study on the ways in which homeschoolers, unschoolers, and other alternative learners have been portrayed in the media, and concluded that these individuals are portrayed generally as geeky, awkward children with overzealous parents. As stated by Houseman, "many members of the general public rarely encounter anyone who subscribes to an alternative method of schooling, and may come to rely on these negative, inauthentic, and potentially harmful media propagated stereotypes to characterize their images of homeschooling (and) unschooling" (p. 16). The smart but unsocialized unschooled character within a movie may be the one individual that pops into a person's head when they hear about unschooling.

Tara Westover's book *Educated* (2018) has also created negative associations toward unschooling for many mainstream readers. Westover was born to survivalists in Idaho, and never set foot into a classroom until was she was in college. For the majority of her life, she was unschooled, and spent time working with her father on their land and in his junkyard. In addition, she assisted in preparing tinctures, oils, and herbs for her mother, a midwife. When she was not working with her parents or family, she was teaching herself the skills she needed to learn to get into college, and later got accepted to Brigham Young University, Harvard University, and Cambridge University. A subplot of *Educated* focuses on the violence she witnessed and received by her brother, and to some readers, unschooling became an easy cover-up for abuse and dysfunction. In reality, "limited evidence shows that home educated children are abused at a lower rate than the general public, and no evidence shows that homeschooled children are at any higher risk of abuse" (Ray, 2018).

Although there have been many criticisms of unschooling published within popular magazines, newspapers, and blogs (Goldstein, 2012; Kozlowska, 2014; Fuglei, 2015) many of those criticisms have never been backed by research, and follow the aforementioned stereotypes. Goldstein states that unschooling "is rooted in distrust of the public sphere, in class privilege, and in the dated presumption that children hail from two-parent families." In reality, as stated previously, there has been a spike in the percentage of homeschooled children reported as poor, with 21% of homeschool families reporting as poor in 2016 (McQuiggan et al.,

2017). Although not the majority, there are numerous single, working parents that also homeschool or unschool (Currie-Knight and Riley, 2019). Fuglei (2015) states that there is publicly expressed worry that the lack of structure inherent in unschooling will make it difficult for students to adjust to schedules and deadlines once they enter college, a myth that was unfounded in Gray and Riley's study of young adult unschoolers (2015). This reliance on myths and stereotypes leads again to a call for increased research on unschoolers and those who choose paths of alternative learning, as well as greater societal understanding of what being unschooled really means.

References

ABC News-Nightline. (2010, June 10). *Extreme parenting: Radical unschooling*. https://www.youtube.com/watch?v=UuhfhRLwTB0.

Alliance for Self Directed Learning (ASDE). (2020). https://www.self-directed.org/.

Currie-Knight, K., & Riley, G. (2019–Present). Gina and Kevin introduce the podcast. [Audio Podcast]. *Learning by Living*. https://www.spreaker.com/show/learning-by-living-podcast.

Dodd, S. (2019). *Terminology*. https://sandradodd.com/terminology.html.

Drummond, R. (2007). *Confessions of a pioneer woman: The relaxed homeschooler*. https://thepioneerwoman.com/homeschooling/the-relaxed-homeschooler/.

Fuglei, M. (2015, January 21). *Unschooling: Inspirational learning method or educational neglect?* https://education.cu-portland.edu/blog/classroom-resources/unschooling/.

Goldstein, D. (2012, February 16). Liberals, don't homeschool your kids. *Slate*. https://slate.com/human-interest/2012/02/homeschooling-and-unschooling-among-liberals-and-progressives.html.

Gray, P., & Riley, G. (2013). The challenges and benefits of unschooling according to 232 families who have chosen that route. *Journal of Unschooling and Alternative Learning, 7*, 1–27.

Griffith, M. (1998). *The unschooling handbook: How to use the whole world as your child's classroom*. Roseville, CA: Prima Publishing.

Hanes, S. (2016, February 14). Free range education: Why the unschooling movement is growing. *The Christian Science Monitor*. https://www.csmonitor.com/USA/Education/2016/0214/Free-range-education-Why-the-unschooling-movement-is-growing.

Hewitt, B. (2014, August 12). We don't need no education. *Outsider Magazine*. https://www.outsideonline.com/1928266/we-dont-need-no-education.

Holt, J. (1977). *Growing Without Schooling, 1*(#1), 1.

Home School Legal Defense Association (HSLDA). (2020). https://hslda.org/content/about/.

Houseman, D. C. (2011). 'Nerdy know it alls' and 'paranoid parents': Images of alternative learning in films and television programs. *Journal of Unschooling and Alternative Learning, 5*, 1–17.

Katz, M. S. (1976). *A history of compulsory education laws*. Bloomington, IN: Phi Delta Kappa.

Kirschner, D. H. (2008). *Producing unschoolers: Learning through living in a U.S. education movement* (Doctoral dissertation). http://repository.upenn.edu/dissertations/AAI3309459.

Kozlowska, H. (2014, August 24). Children need free play, but are unschoolers giving them too much? *The New York Times—Op Ed*. https://op-talk.blogs.nytimes.com/2014/08/24/children-need-free-play-but-are-unschoolers-giving-them-too-much/.

Martin-Chang, S. L., & Gould, O. N. (2011). The impact of schooling on academic achievement: Evidence from homeschooled and traditionally schooled students. *Canadian Journal of Behavioral Science, 43*, 195–202.

Martin, D. (2013a, February 4). The radical unschooling life with Joe and Dayna Martin [Video]. *You Tube*. https://www.youtube.com/watch?v=HmZueW6Bwz4.

Martin, D. (2013b, July 9). My family on ABC's hit show "Wife Swap" [Video]. *Dayna Martin*. http://daynamartin.com/unschooling-blog/wife-swap/.

McBroom, B. (2012, November 6). Things that hold unschooling back. *Pottery and Pastry*. https://brennamcbroom.wordpress.com/2012/11/06/things-that-hold-unschooling-back/.

McDonald, K. (2019, July 8). *Unschooling: Shifting from force to freedom in education. Unschooling and the rights of children*. https://www.cato-unbound.org/2019/07/08/kerry-mcdonald/unschooling-shifting-force-freedom-education.

McGraw, P. (2011). *The great school debate: Dayna, Joe, unschoolers*. https://www.drphil.com/slideshows/great-school-debate-dayna-joe-unschoolers/.

McQuiggan, M., Megra, M., & Grady, S. (2017). Parent and family involvement in education: Results from the National Household Education Surveys Program of 2016. Washington, DC: National Center for Education Statistics.

National Home Education Research Institute (NHERI). (2020). https://www.nheri.org/.

Olsen, N. (2020). What is radical unschooling? *Unschoolers.org*. https://unschoolers.org/radical-unschooling/what-is-radical-unschooling/.

Ray, B. (2018). *Child abuse of public, private, and homeschooled students: Evidence, philosophy, and reason*. https://www.nheri.org/child-abuse-of-public-school-private-school-and-homeschool-students-evidence-philosophy-and-reason/.

Ricci, C. (2012). *The willed curriculum, unschooling, and self direction: What do love, trust, respect, care, and compassion have to do with learning*. Toronto, ON: Ricci Publishing.

Westover, T. (2018). *Educated*. New York: Penguin Random House Publishers.

Wisconsin vs. Yoder (1972, May 15). 406. U.S. 205. https://supreme.justia.com/cases/federal/us/406/205/.

CHAPTER 6

Paths to Unschooling

It is always interesting to explore the ways in which individuals and families make the decision to unschool. In Gray and Riley's study of 232 unschooling families, participants described numerous paths to unschooling, including previous experiences within formal school, a period of structured homeschooling, an interest in natural parenting and natural family living, a philosophy of life or learning, and information gained from books, online resources, speakers, conferences, or other unschooling families. Usually, it was a combination of these things (2013).

Previous School Experience

Within the Gray and Riley (2013) study, almost 44% of families indicated that a child's previous experience in school led them to choose unschooling. Some families took their children out of school because of the overall environment of the school and/or specific school rules. Because public and private schools serve hundreds of students, most school rules are inflexible and are instituted to manage large groups of children or teens. These rules are helpful for overall structure and order, but not helpful for children or teens who want to be more autonomous in their behavior or their learning. Other families in Gray and Riley's (2013) study referred to the wasted time in school, the child's boredom in school, or a loss of curiosity and interest in learning that they saw after their child

G. Riley, *Unschooling*, Palgrave Studies in Alternative Education,
https://doi.org/10.1007/978-3-030-49292-2_6

began attending school. As an example, a recent Gallop poll illustrates that there is a steady decline in student engagement and motivation as a child goes from late elementary to high school. Seventy-four percent of traditionally schooled fifth graders reported being engaged in their classes at school, while only thirty-two percent of traditionally schooled high school juniors did (Calderon and Yu, 2017).

A small percentage of participants in Gray and Riley's study referred to their child being bullied or having experienced depression, anxiety, or other mental health issues while enrolled in school (2013), a not uncommon occurrence (World Health Organization, 2020). Some parents tried desperately to have their child find happiness in public or private schooling, letting go after finding that the system really wasn't working for their child or teen. As Laura Grace Weldon reflects:

> When the time came for kindergarten, we put our firstborn in school as we did with our next three children. I clung to the hope that institutions can be changed from within. I volunteered in classrooms, headed committees, worked with a parent group to bring artists to the school, and advocated to keep corporate influence out of the schools. But when you're stuck in the system, you end up enforcing the same structure you're railing against if your kids are to "succeed" in that system. Worse, school didn't really work for my kids....Our five-year-old could read well but still had to complete endless pre-reading assignments along with his kindergarten class; our eight-year-old's teacher kept insisting he be medicated for ADHD symptoms we never saw outside of school; our eleven-year-old was expected to do grade-level busywork although she tested at high school and college levels; and our 14-year-old was bored by AP classes and one of many kids hassled by a few bullies at school. (2018, p. 6)

A period of unschooling can be healing for a student who has struggled in public or private school, as unschooling brings a student back to a place where they can be fully themselves. There is no pretense, and little peer pressure. Institution-based expectations are dropped, allowing the student to focus on the things they love and are truly interested in. As one parent describes:

> Last spring, my husband and I pulled our eighth-grade son out of a private, academically focused school that he had attended since pre-K. While it was a major decision, it was also an effortless one. We had reached the end of our rope. Immediately after the change, all the friction, drama, and

> tension of the past 8 years melted away. And it kept getting better. Over the remainder of the spring and into the summer my son and husband forged a deep bond, spending most of their time together, hanging out, talking, doing guy stuff. Without school in the way, our family grew closer and our son regained his passion for art and athletics. (Keller, 2014)

Deschooling

Grace Llewelyn, author of *The Teenage Liberation Handbook*, reminds parents to be gentle with individuals transitioning from school to unschooling, and states, "Before you can start your new way of life, you have to let the old one go" (1998, p. 131). This letting go many times involves a process of "deschooling," or allowing the child or teen to decompress from the structures and traditions of school. For some, this may mean an extended period of sitting home, resting, reading, writing, journaling, reflecting, or even just watching television and playing video games. For others, this may mean spending more time in the outside world, working, volunteering, or being with friends, neighbors, or family members. As Todd (2019) expresses "Deschooling has the potential to instill a different ethic of self, identity, freedom, spontaneity, discovery, curiosity, etc., thus creating arrangements of power that are productive, not oppressive, and (which) preserve individual freedom and autonomy." Deschooling permits the child or teen to form a new identity, not as a student enrolled in a school, but as a person living and learning within a home and community. No longer is the individual bound by their classroom or their teachers' or peers' expectations of them. Instead, the child has the freedom to be their own person, creating renewed relationships with the people around them, including their parent or parents.

Interestingly, it is not only the child or teen that goes through a period of deschooling. Many unschooling parents state that they have to go through the process too. For example, parents will state that they needed to let go of traditional ideas about academic achievement, academic success, homework, and structure in order to truly embrace the unschooling process (Hunt, 2020). While deschooling, one realizes that there is no pick up time, or no specific time they have to get their children on the bus. There is no homework or school-sponsored activities, because all work and learning is already done at home. Any academic, social, or emotional success their children experience while unschooling does not lead to time on the honor roll, good report cards, certificates of achievement, or high GPA's. Parents need to get used to the fact that they most likely will be with their children twenty-four hours per day. It is an adjustment, and for some parents, it is not an easy one. Unschooling creates a different, more intrinsically motivated environment for learning. Success does not come from a place of external validation. Instead, a sense of accomplishment is felt and experienced from within, for both child and parent. As one parent in the Gray and Riley (2013) study shared "Our own experiences in school, college, and graduate school taught us to only value humans by their degrees on a wall. We now realize there is a more to a human than that."

Unschooling After a Period of Homeschooling

For many families within Gray and Riley's (2013) study of unschooling families, unschooling came after a period of homeschooling, or "school at home." Sometimes the shift to unschooling occurred when children or teens resisted the use of a state or set curriculum, or when utilizing the curriculum was causing stress in the home. Others realized that they noticed their children doing much more learning when the curriculum wasn't used. For example, a parent within the Gray and Riley (2013) study shared:

> During my daughter's sixth grade year, our first year of homeschooling, we did school at home following a traditional homeschool curriculum. We changed curriculum materials several times, nothing seemed to be working very well. I stumbled across unschooling on the internet during that first year, while searching for better curriculum materials. I checked out every book I could find on the inter-library loan system that referenced unschooling…the whole philosophy just made so much sense to me.

Currie-Knight and Riley (2019) found this shift from a period of formal homeschooling to unschooling to be a common trend when interviewing unschooling parents on their podcast *Learning by Living*. In interviewing writer Kerry McDonald, a story was shared of her daughter starting kindergarten, which propelled McDonald to search for curriculum that was going to be both fun and engaging. As she was finalizing curriculum choices, her daughter taught herself how to read. This is when McDonald realized that there was a different way of doing things. Laura Grace

Weldon (2018) also reports this phenomenon when describing her family's journey to unschooling:

> Initially I leaned toward a project-based approach. To my dismay, I carried some school-like attitudes into the process. Although I thought I was encouraging my kids to follow their interests and explore related areas within that framework, it didn't go over all that well with my eight-year-old...He would repeatedly drop a pencil to crawl after it on the floor, or stare out the window instead of completing the project I thought he wanted to work on. It didn't matter if we were going to the park as soon as he was done, he just didn't want to finish. His inner voice insisted on a larger integrity. He needed to learn as he most naturally learned. (p. 94)

For many new homeschooling parents, "school at home" seems to be what they are supposed to be doing. A majority of states and school districts require it, asking parents to take attendance, use textbooks and printed curriculum, and give (or have someone else proctor) standardized assessments. However, very quickly, parents learn that it is almost impossible to bring grade-based classroom learning, created for large groups of children, into a home environment. Academic development and growth are not always linear, and individuals have unique strengths and interests. A healthy learning environment is not one where a child sits at a desk all day, reading a textbook and completing workbook pages and artificial laboratory-based assignments. Children and teens, given the opportunity, naturally know what they want to do and want to learn. Unschooling provides a child with an environmental condition in which they can thrive.

This is not to say that unschooling works for everyone. It is a choice, out of a myriad of educational choices, including public, private and charter schools. Some students will thrive in more structured, grade-based classrooms. They enjoy receiving extrinsic rewards, praise, and grades for their work, and they are good at it. They love being surrounded by children or teens their same age. They enjoy working for their teachers and seeing staff and administrators. They excel in the built-in after school activities schools provide. For others, school is a welcome escape from a tumultuous home environment. It is a place where they can escape a difficult, crowded, or confusing environment at home and have space and peace to think, learn, and have fun. School may be, for some, the only place where they get a hot or balanced meal. It may provide an escape.

In these situations, school is the right fit, and those choices should be honored and supported.

Parent's Own Previous Experience with Formal Schooling

When one attends school for an extended period, the experience of school is something that shapes and molds them, sometimes in a positive way, other times in a negative or neutral way. In Gray and Riley's study of unschooling families (2013), nearly 32% of participants referred to their own negative experience with school as a motivation to unschool their own children. One participant in the study directly stated "My K-12 experience was the unhappiest time of my life" (p.17). Another participant expressed that she and her husband knew they wanted to homeschool after years of experiencing bullying, harassment, and shame within the traditional school environment. An additional study has also found that past school experiences can be a motivation to unschool. For example, within Morrison's 2016 study of unschooling mothers, one parent stated "From my whole school experience I was always trying to please my teachers, please my parents…To this day I don't know what I did for me. What I did was for someone else, and I think that really helped me learn that I didn't want my daughter to live that kind of a life" (p. 59). Traditional school experiences and memories stay with people, and those who have had an especially hard time, or just pursued success for someone or something else, may want something different for their children.

Interestingly, some unschooling parents have backgrounds in public education, educational policy, or higher education. These parents are familiar with the landscape of school and have chosen a different path for their children, based on what is best for their family structure. Their experiences within the classroom and understanding of learning theories, educational theories, and pedagogical best practices have given them the courage to choose a less formal path of learning, one that is student-directed and full of play and exploration (Morrison, 2016). Parents like these also may have the intellectual, academic, and economic resources to be able to provide their children with this type of free choice, play-based environment.

Unschooling and Natural Family Living

Some individuals find unschooling because of their interest or experience in attachment parenting or natural family living (Gray and Riley, 2013). Within Morrison's study, many mothers who chose to unschool had already experienced the power that can come directly from the home. Some of these parents had their babies at home or practiced attachment parenting. Others grew food in their gardens or were dedicated to cooking most meals at home. These mothers found confidence in what they could do within the home, making unschooling feel like a natural next step (2016). Rebecca English's qualitative study of reasons for choosing homeschooling in Australia concluded that "there was a link between the mother's identification with attachment parenting and their decision to home educate. In particular, the following of an attachment parenting philosophy and the choice of unschooling were deeply emmeshed" (English, 2015, p. 12).

The organization La Leche League (LLL) has also brought some to unschooling, albeit indirectly. LLL's official mission is to "To help mothers worldwide to breastfeed through mother-to-mother support, encouragement, information, and education, and to promote a better understanding of breastfeeding as an important element in the healthy development of the baby and mother" (La Leche League, 2020). However, many LLL members would agree that LLL also brings a new perspective on motherhood and parenting. As recognized in Bender and Taves, LLL does not explicitly advocate homeschooling or unschooling, but encourages parents to make heart-based decisions centered on their individual child's needs (2012). Making these heart-centered choices may involve taking an alternative educational path.

Nancy Plent shared her experience in finding homeschooling through LLL within an essay in *Life Learning Magazine* (2020), expressing, "My introduction to homeschooling was through La Leche League, and I admired the families around me who learned together. For me, their parenting philosophy could be summed up in three words – these parents were loving, kind and respectful in their interactions with their children."

Parental philosophy also plays a role in a family's decision to unschool, and it is difficult to surmise whether it is the actual parental philosophy that comes first, or whether the thought of unschooling creates a different sort of parent/child relationship. Unschooling tends to lend itself to a more collaborative parenting style, as by nature, children are spending more time with their parent(s). Additionally, much of that time, for the parent(s), is spent following their child's lead, instead of the other way around. As Dr. Carlo Ricci, unschooling pioneer and founder of the *Journal of Unschooling and Alternative Learning* articulates:

> As an unschooling family, my children have never been punished. They have never experienced timeouts or any other form of externally imposed directive. They are treated with love, trust, respect, care, and compassion. This does not mean that we never disagree, but when we disagree, we deal with it in democratic ways usually through dialogue and conversation. This has given me tremendous respect for how capable young people are. (2011, p. 3)

Morrison expands on this by explaining that most unschooling environments inherently provide children with lots of personal autonomy and play, as well as opportunities for supportive collaborations. The unschooling home is usually not authoritarian or authoritative in philosophy (2016). Instead, it is a home in which there is a strong sense of trust in children, and their ideas and motivations.

Once a parent does experience unschooling, it seems that their philosophy of life and education changes and alters, much like John Holt's philosophy of education changed in the 1970s. Some parents who experience an unschooled environment and see children thriving in freedom, also change their minds about other things, including, but not limited the rights of children (Ricci, 2011), the role of institutions in society, and the role of the environment. When individuals let go of their preconceptions about existing structures, not limited to school, many new learnings, interests, and thoughts come forth, initiating a change in overall worldview (Cooper and Sureau, 2007).

Books Influencing Unschooling

When asked about influences when it came to the decision to unschool, a majority of respondents in the Gray and Riley (2013) survey of unschooling families mentioned books. The author that influenced participants most, by over half the respondents in the survey, was John Holt. Holt's most popular books, *How Children Fail* (1964) and *How Children Learn* (1967) are classics in education, and *Growing Without Schooling*

(1977–2001) was instrumental in forming a sense of community for individuals who decided to educate their children at home. Thanks to Pat Farenga, *Growing Without Schooling* still exists as an online resource for unschooling parents throughout the world.

John Taylor Gatto's books, *Dumbing Us Down: The Hidden Curriculum of a Contemporary Society* (1992) and *The Underground History of American Education* (2001) also struck a chord with many parents in their exploration of unschooling. Perhaps it was because Gatto spent thirty years as a teacher in the New York City public school system, admitted the system was broken, and saw unschooling, homeschooling, and democratic schooling as ways for students to really learn. *Dumbing Us Down* (1992) is a collection of Gatto's speeches, promoting the opinion that school creates emotionally and intellectually dependent children with little autonomy. *The Underground History of American Education* (2001) discusses the original purpose of public schools, which, in Gatto's opinion, was to maintain social order and restrict power to a select number of people. Gatto experienced firsthand what it was like to be a teacher trying to change a system from within, a system that frequently rejects institutional change. He saw how the students within that system suffered. It takes a brave person to point out flaws in a system many embrace, and Gatto, for many parents, became a champion of alternative education; an experienced teacher who understood why parents would keep their children out of the traditional classroom. Sandra Dodd, an unschooling parent, author, and advocate, was the third most mentioned influence in Gray and Riley's (2013) study. Dodd is the owner of sandradodd.com, a website devoted to unschooling. Parents turn to Dodd for personal stories and webpages dedicated to all things unschooling and home learning.

Also mentioned as influential, among other writers, were Alfie Kohn and Grace Llewellen. Kohn is best known as the author of *Punished by Rewards: The Trouble with Gold Stars, Incentive Plans, A's, Praise, and Other Bribes* (1999), but has also written many other books and hundreds of articles focusing on the disadvantages of extrinsically motivated learning and the great advantages of intrinsically motivated learning. Although not directly a proponent of unschooling (2005), Kohn does want us to rethink societal views on learning and schooling, and push back on a purely standards and achievement-focused culture. He also feels strongly about instituting interest-based curriculums, and getting rid of mandatory homework within schools (Kohn, 2019).

Grace Llewellen, author of *The Teenage Liberation Handbook: How to Quit School and Get a Real Life and Education* (1998), has influenced many adolescents in their quest to seek alternatives to school. The book itself is divided into four parts: why some teens should consider leaving school, how to make preparations to leave, what to do academically after leaving school, and finding viable employment that is motivating and enjoyable. In his reflection of Llewellen's work, Jodah (2017) affirms, "As a teenager struggling with many issues, including bullying, social isolation and poverty, I concluded that school was largely contributing to my misery -thanks to this book, I finally had the clarity and courage to leave school" (p. 1). Through her writing, Llewellen has given teens a tangible way to thrive and grow outside a traditional learning environment. She has also given parents and educators a plan to think about different ways teens can learn outside of school.

Conferences and Speakers

Many parents mentioned that their resolve or path to unschool was influenced by attending unschooling conferences and hearing speakers talk about alternatives to traditional school (Gray and Riley, 2013). Conferences like the Life is Good Unschooling Conference and the Alternative Education Resource Organization (AERO) conference allow parents and families the opportunity to hear varied speakers and proponents of unschooling discuss their experiences and knowledge regarding alternative educational choices. More importantly, conferences allow unschooling families to spend time with one another, laughing, playing, and sharing stories of their educational journeys. Conferences are sometimes the very first time parents are exposed to what unschooling is and how it works, and hearing experts talk about logistics, research, and personal experiences makes the choice all the more real and do-able.

For those who cannot personally attend conferences due to travel, time, or budget restrictions, recorded Technology, Education, and Design (TED) talks create a compelling alternative. Sir Ken Robinson's 2006 TED Talk, watched over 50 million times, entitled "Do Schools Kill Creativity?", is one of the more popular talks for those interested in school options. Sir Ken Robinson is an author, speaker, and national education consultant and reformer. His "Do Schools Kill Creativity?" TED talk focused on calling for a different way to look at intelligence and learning. He also discussed embracing creativity as an invaluable asset and educating the whole child. Many saw his talk as an obvious affirmation of the world of alternative education. Although in 2006 Robinson wasn't promoting homeschooling or unschooling, he is currently an advocate for nontraditional education (Reilly, 2018), and is someone who practices what he preaches. He allowed his daughter to leave high school at 16 to engage in a self-directed curriculum and encourages others to consider which educational option, including leaving school, may be best for their children (Reilly, 2018).

Peter Gray's TED Talk "How Our Schools Thwart Our Passions" (2018) has also inspired parents to unschool their child. Gray's TED talk mentions Kirsten Olsen's book *Wounded by School: Recapturing the Joy in Learning and Standing Up to Old School Culture* (2009), a book focused on school reform and the healing of school-based wounds. Within his speech, Gray discusses the common school practice of decreasing recess and increasing standardized testing, which he believes leads to greater societal issues like a decline of creative thinking in school-aged children and a surge in childhood and adolescent levels of mental illness. Twenge and Foster (2010) attribute the increase in cases of depression and anxiety in college students to young adults feeling loss of control and decreased autonomy over their own lives. They then theorize that this may be due to a societal shift from intrinsic goals like happiness and familial closeness to more extrinsic goals such as a high socioeconomic status or physical attractiveness. Gray (2010) hypothesizes that the increased levels of depression and anxiety documented in high school and college students is caused by a decrease in free play and an increase of time at school.

Play allows children to explore and learn, many times without adult supervision or direction. Play also grants children time to figure out what they like and dislike and where their passions and interest lie. Within his TED talk, Gray talks about his brother, who left school at a young age, found his passion for the guitar and other stringed instruments, and later became an internationally renowned luthier. He ends by declaring, "If we want our children to grow up with passionate interests, we have to find an alternative to school…at least an alternative to school as we know it today" (2018).

Other Unschooling Families

Lastly, meeting other unschooling families within one's community served as a path to unschooling (Gray and Riley, 2013), and gave parents the courage to choose to unschool their own children (Fensham-Smith,

2019). It is one thing to read about unschooling in a book, and quite another to talk to parent(s) nearby actually doing it. Lois (2012) notes the importance of these conversations and also of the feelings of relief found in sharing challenges and criticisms that come from making an alternative choice. Within the unschooling community, support is important, and the encouragement of those who have made a similar choice is invaluable.

References

Alternative Education Resource Organization. (2020). https://www.aeroconference.org/.

Bender, C., & Taves, A. (Eds.). (2012). *What matters: Ethnographies of value in a not so secular age*. New York: Columbia University Press.

Calderon, V. J., & Yu, D. (2017, June 1). Student enthusiasm falls as high school graduation nears. *Gallup*. https://news.gallup.com/opinion/gallup/211631/student-enthusiasm-falls-high-school-graduation-nears.aspx.

Cooper, B. S., & Sureau, J. (2007). The politics of homeschooling: New developments, new challenges. *Educational Policy, 21*(1), 110–131.

Currie-Knight, K., & Riley, G. (Host). (2019–Present). Journalist and parent to four unschoolers with Kerry McDonald. [Audio Podcast]. *Learning by Living*. https://www.spreaker.com/user/learningbyliving/02-kerry-mcdonald.

Dodd, S. (2020). Sandradodd.com.

English, R. (2015). Use your freedom of choice: Reasons for choosing homeschool in Australia. *Journal of Unschooling and Alternative Learning, 9*, 1–18.

Fensham-Smith, A. (2019). Becoming a home educator in a networked world: Towards the democratization of educational alternatives? *Other Education, 8*, 27–57.

Gatto, J. T. (1992). *Dumbing us down: The hidden curriculum of compulsory schooling*. Philadelphia: New Society Publishers.

Gatto, J. T. (2001). *The underground history of American education: A schoolteacher's intimate investigation into the problem of modern schooling*. New York: Oxford Village Press.

Gray, P. (2010, January 26). The decline of play and the rise of children's mental disorders. *Freedom to Learn. Psychology Today*. https://www.psychologytoday.com/us/blog/freedom-learn/201001/the-decline-play-and-rise-in-childrens-mental-disorders.

Gray, P. (2018). *How schools thwart our passions*. https://www.youtube.com/watch?v=coMXLy8RBIc.

Gray, P., & Riley, G. (2013). The challenges and benefits of unschooling according to 232 families who have chosen that route. *Journal of Unschooling and Alternative Learning, 7*, 1–27.

Griffith, M. (1998). *The unschooling handbook: How to use the whole world as your child's classroom*. Roseville, CA: Prima Publishing.

Growing Without Schooling. (1977–2001). https://www.johnholtgws.com/.

Holt, J. (1964). *How children fail*. New York: Pitman Publishing Company.

Holt, J. (1967). *How children learn*. New York: Pitman Publishing Company.

Hunt, J. (2020). Deschooling a parent: Learning to trust. *The Natural Child Project*. https://www.naturalchild.org/articles/jan_hunt/deschooling.html.

Jodah, M. (2017). Unschooling and how I became liberated: The teenage liberation handbook, quitting school, and getting a real life and education. *Journal of Unschooling and Alternative Learning, 11*, 1–7.

Keller, A. (2014, February 11). How to unschool a kid and send him to school. *Penelope Trunk Blog*. https://education.penelopetrunk.com/2014/02/11/how-to-unschool-a-struggling-student/.

Kohn, A. (1999). *Punished by rewards: The trouble with gold stars, incentive plans, A's, praise, and other bribes*. New York: Houghton Mifflin.

Kohn, A. (2005, August). *The trouble with pure freedom: A case for active adult involvement in progressive education*. Keynote presentation at the Alternative Education Resource Organization (AERO) conference, Long Island, NY.

Kohn, A. (2019, September 3). 'Should grades be based on classwork?' and other questions we should stop asking. *Education Week*. https://www.edweek.org/ew/articles/2019/09/04/should-grades-be-based-on-classwork-and.html.

La Leche League. (2020). https://www.llli.org/.

Life is Good Unschooling Conference. (2020). http://lifeisgoodconference.com/.

Llewelyn, G. (1998). *The teenage liberation handbook: How to quit school and get a real life and education*. Eugene, OR: Lowry House Publishing.

Lois, J. (2012). *Home is where the school is: The logic of home-schooling and the emotional labor of mothering*. New York: New York University Press.

Morrison, K. (2016). The courage to let them play: Factors influencing and limiting feelings of self-efficacy in unschooling mothers. *Journal of Unschooling and Alternative Learning, 16*, 1–34.

Olsen, K. (2009). *Wounded by school: Recapturing the joy in learning and standing up to old school culture*. New York: Teachers College Press.

Plent, N. (2002). Passionate about unschooling in New Jersey. *Life Learning Magazine*. http://www.lifelearningmagazine.com/0712/nancy_plent_passionate_about_unschooling_in_New_Jersey.htm.

Reilly, K. (2018, March 26). Why dropping out of school could actually help your kid, according to one education expert. *Time Magazine*. https://time.com/5201227/ken-robinson-children-drop-out-school/.

Ricci, C. (2011). Unschooling and the willed curriculum. *Encounter: Education for Meaning and Social Justice* (pp. 45–48). https://great-ideas.org/Encounter/Ricci243.pdf.

Robinson, K. (2006). Do schools kill creativity? [Video]. *TED Conferences*. https://www.ted.com/talks/sir_ken_robinson_do_schools_kill_creativity?language=en#t-2107.

Todd, J. D. (2019, September 26). From deschooling to unschooling: Rethinking anarchopedagogy after Ivan Illich. *Tipping Points: Alliance for Self-Directed Education*. https://www.self-directed.org/tp/from deschooling-to-unschooling/.

Twenge, J. M., & Foster, J. D. (2010). Birth cohort increases in narcissistic personality traits among American college students, 1982–2009. *Social Psychology and Personality Science, 1*, 99–106.

Weldon, L. G. (2018). Unexpected path to free range learning. *Journal of Unschooling and Alternative Learning, 12*, 1–18.

World Health Organization. (2020). *Adolescent mental health fact sheet*. https://www.who.int/news-room/fact-sheets/detail/adolescent-mental-health.

CHAPTER 7

Subject-Based Learning in Unschooling

One of the most common questions asked of unschooling families is "How do children learn if there is no set curriculum?" This question presupposes that children cannot learn without external reinforcement and is emblematic of contemporary society's views regarding the capabilities of children. In short, we as a society have let go of the idea that children can learn on their own, without adult interference. We hold fast to the belief that children and adolescents need teachers, expensive technology, and long days at school to learn what they need to learn, even when evidence proves otherwise. Unschoolers show us that learning without direct instruction is possible.

Learning to Read

Teachers spend a significant amount of instructional time in the primary grades teaching students how to read. In many schools, phonetics, decoding, sight word recognition, and comprehension are all explicitly taught and reviewed. However, despite this intensive intervention, scores in reading are plummeting across the nation (Camera, 2019). When students don't learn to read in a specified time, usually by age seven, they are sent for formal evaluation to a psychologist or psychiatrist for a diagnosis of dyslexia or another reading difficulty. What if, however, reading was seen as a natural process instead of something to be formally taught? What if there was no correct age for learning to read? The field

G. Riley, *Unschooling*, Palgrave Studies in Alternative Education,
https://doi.org/10.1007/978-3-030-49292-2_7

of emergent literacy proposes that children gain knowledge of reading and writing even before they are developmentally ready to read and write words. According to Lancy et al., (2014), cultural transmission may be at work here too. Cultural transmission happens without teaching, and is a way of learning and passing on information through familial or cultural norms. What if reading was seen as a cultural practice as well as a cognitive skill?

In 2010, Peter Gray wrote an article on his blog, *Freedom to Learn*, based on an unofficial study of eighteen unschoolers. In surveying these unschoolers, he came up with seven principles that provided some understanding about how individuals learn to read without formal schooling. Included within these principles are the ideas that there is no critical period for learning to read; that intrinsically motivated, non-dyslexic children can go from nonreading to fluent reading quickly; and that reading may be socially learned through shared participation in activities that involve books and words.

In 2013, Dr. Karl Wheatley published an article within the *Journal of Unschooling and Alternative Learning* describing how his children learned to read without formal instruction. Within this article, he also asserts that taking a deeper look at the unschooling process can help reframe thoughts about traditional education, learning, and teaching as a whole, including mainstream ideas regarding how children learn to read. This thought was also reiterated in work by Csoli (2013), who reflected on how tenets of what she termed "natural learning" could also be helpful when instructing children with learning disabilities.

Harriet Pattison (2016) provided the first major study of how children learned to read outside an institutionalized setting. The families in her study practiced different forms of home education, including unschooling. In her study, 311 home-educating parents were surveyed on how their children learned to read. Although some parents explicitly taught their children how to read, other parents took a less formal role in teaching reading. Some did not teach their children at all, allowing reading to develop organically.

In May of 2016, the author of this book was awarded a grant to research how unschoolers learned to read. In 2018, the results of this study were published in the *Journal of Unschooling and Alternative Learning*. Twenty-eight unschooled adults (age 18 and older) were surveyed and asked to recall their experiences with reading and learning to read. Through these responses, the author explored how reading can be learned naturally without adult intervention; and how this may affect later motivation for reading, writing, and other academic endeavors.

Overall Experience with Books

In the aforementioned survey, participants were asked to recall and discuss their overall experience with books or printed literature as a child. Specifically, participants were asked (a) if there were books in their home; (b) if they recall being read to; and (c) if they recalled seeing the adults around them read. The root of the question was based on current research measuring the effect of number of books in the home on subsequent academic achievement (Evans et al., 2010). According to Evans et al., having a five hundred book library, especially in families who are considered low in socioeconomic status, can boost a child's reading level up approximately 3.2 years. Even having twenty plus books in the home increases a child's reading success (2010).

Within the study of unschoolers learning to read, in every case, participants reported there being books in the home, and the majority expressed that there were lots of books in their home. Libraries were mentioned frequently as an additional source of books and each participant also recalled being read to each and every day. A majority of participants (20 participants; or 71.4%) specifically mentioned witnessing adults around them read. As an example, one participant reminisced:

> Our home was always full of books. My mum and dad always had books they were reading personally, and mum would read to us individually and read chapter books to all us kids together. Mom would also often read to us in the car when we went on a holiday. We visited the library often and would go to bookstores as a treat, with everyone being able to choose a book.

Reading aloud is a powerful literacy technique. It increases vocabulary development, enhances fluency, boosts oral language skills, and develops critical thinking skills. It allows children and teens the time to process text and ask questions about the text. It also motivates students to become more engaged in reading (Johnson, 2015). Reading aloud also creates an emotional connection between the reader and the person listening. That emotional connection can evoke later positive memories and associations around reading and books as a whole.

How Unschoolers Learned to Read

Another question in the survey asked if participants recalled how they learned to read. Out of 28 respondents, nine were coded as "taught" in some way. This referred to learning based on facilitation, either by a parent, family member, or other. The facilitation could have been formal, through the use of workbooks or flashcards, or informal, through the use of games. The same participants that were coded as "taught" also considered themselves relaxed homeschoolers as opposed to unschoolers or radical unschoolers.

Those who were coded as "taught" either had parents who would review basic phonemes with them, or facilitate a whole language approach to reading. For example, one participant stated, "I know my sister learned to read on rollerskates. She's a kinesthetic learner. My mom would hold up phonics cards and my sister would do laps around the kitchen table and on skates and read one card per round." Another participant shared:

> I remember spending nights with my mother slowly reading words with help…learning how a few basic letters sounded so I could get half the word right before needing her help for the rest. My little sister was trying to learn too…I didn't like when she was doing well. I remember going to bed alone one night frustrated with the situation with my sister. I picked up the book and tried reading. I remember it feeling magical. I could read the basic book we were learning with! The words that looked alien before suddenly made sense in my brain. (Riley, 2018)

In 46.4% of respondents, reading seemed to happen naturally, with little to no teaching or facilitation. For example, one participant said: "There was no rote learning, phonics, or memorization involved. I learned to read the way a child learns to speak – by doing and observing it. My parents read to me a lot, and I assume I picked up reading in that way" (Riley, 2018). This is very different from what happens in most public schools, where students are explicitly taught letters, sounds, and decoding skills, and given assigned leveled text to read. Pattison (2016) notes that maybe the "reading naturally" we see in unschooled students denotes that reading is more a cultural practice instead of a cognitive skill, as cultural transmission happens without teaching. As an example, another participant wrote:

> I had a favorite book that I would have my parents read aloud to me as often as possible. But sometimes they were busy and there was no one to read it to me. So I tried to memorize the story. I remember taking this book and pouring over each page, telling myself the story over and over – and then listening intently to my parents when they read aloud until I pretty much had it memorized. One day I had the book open and I was paging through it, it was about halfway through the book that I realized I was no longer relying on my memory to tell me what happened on each page, but instead I was actively reading the words on paper. I ran upstairs and told my mom that I could read! I went immediately to other books, and went a bit slower through them, as I hadn't mastered all the words/sounds yet, but I definitely felt like I'd unlocked the key to reading. (Riley, 2018)

For a small number of the participants in this study, reading was a struggle. As one participant expressed: "I remember it being a slow, frustrating process. It didn't come quickly or naturally to me. I very much wanted to be able to read but learning was not fun" (Riley, 2018). These participants did not report a diagnosis of a reading disability such as dyslexia. However, they admitted that reading did not come easy to them, just as specific subjects may not come easy to some schooled children. This is important to acknowledge, especially considering the myth of the unschooled genius, or the false assumption that parents choose unschooling for their child because they are intellectually or creatively exceptional (Houseman, 2011).

Age of Reading

The survey also asked the question "At approximately what age did you learn to read?" Answers ranged from age 3 through the "early teen years." Out of 28 participants, four participants reported reading before the age of 5, fourteen participants reported reading between the age of 5 and 7.0, five participants reported reading between the age of 7.1 and 8.0. Two participants reported being over 8, and one reported learning to read in their early teens. Two other participants reported that they couldn't recall the exact age they learned to read.

When a student isn't reading before the age of 7 in a public school, an evaluation for special education is considered, specifically for possible classification of a learning disability. However, for nonschooled children, there may be no critical period or best age for learning to read (Gray, 2010).

This does not mean unschooled parents do not worry about their children not learning to read, as almost 18% of participants did remember parents showing some concern over their child not reading at a specific age. One participant shared "I remember numerous times being really anxious or ashamed of myself because girls younger than me were reading better than me. I felt bad, but it almost made me want to learn more" (Riley, 2018). Another participant related that his grandmother showed concern regarding his lack of ability to read and offered money to him for every book he would attempt to read (Riley, 2018). However, a large majority of unschooling parents knew that when their child was ready to read, they would. As one person in the study relayed:

> My parents were not worried about it at all, and neither were my older brothers. We were in a community with a lot of other homeschooled kids at the time, and no one thought it was any big deal. Actually, people kind of took care of the kids that didn't read yet, in a really thoughtful way. They would make sure that kids who didn't read or write yet did not get put on the spot. Also, if anyone needed a scribe to write down stories or ideas, there was always a parent or older sibling to help do that. (Riley, 2018)

Motivation to Read

When discussing what motivated participants to read, participants gave varied responses. Sometimes, it was family members that motivated individuals by positive reinforcement. Other times, the motivation to read was purely intrinsic. Over seventy-eight percent of participants appreciated how unschooling allowed them to learn at their own pace and in their own way, only reading books that they themselves chose. For example, one participant shared "When I was 12, I was reading The Lord of the Rings while my schooled peers were being told which books were 'appropriate' for their reading level. No book was off limits to me…and I think this is a big difference in how I learned to read in comparison to others" (Riley, 2018). Another participant stated, "I think being allowed to lean on my own timing has allowed me to develop other parts of my brain that work really well….and (allowed me to) enjoy something that I may not have if I was forced into it" (Riley, 2018).

Reading and Its Connection to Writing

Participants in the study were also asked if learning to read enhanced their interest in or motivation for writing. This question was asked because within traditional education, learning to read and learning to write are seen as complementary skills. Fifty-two point two percent of individuals who responded to the question stated that reading did indeed assist in developing their writing skills. As one participant shared "I write a lot of poetry now, and that certainly came from my early experiences in reading poetry". Twenty-four percent of participants felt that reading and writing were separate endeavors, or that their learning to write came before learning to read. For example, a participant stated:

> Actually, I would say that it was the other way around. My mom treated words as very important. We often made books together and she wrote down rhymes I made up or stories I told. We learned different ways to bind books. We even had an artist friend come over and show us how to make paper and how to stitch or staple pages together. I think that making my 'writing' into books....was part of what helped me learn to read. As I wrote down the letters and words (sometimes just one or two word phrases), I was actually learning to sound things out. I was never required to do this. We just had all these materials around and everyone was reading and writing and had stories to tell. (Riley, 2018)

Another twenty-four percent of participants answered in a way that implied "maybe," meaning they did not connect a relationship between the two. As an example, a participant wrote "I love to write. I'm not sure if that related to my reading until I was older, though. I don't necessarily connect the two because I like to write nonfiction, and I mostly prefer to read fiction, and I think the styles are very different (although perhaps they shouldn't be)" (Riley, 2018).

Major Findings of the Unschooling and Reading Study

One of the most noteworthy conclusions that came out of this study was that most unschoolers believe that learning, and particularly learning to read, can happen naturally, without adult interference. Another significant finding is that most of the unschoolers participating in this study grew up in environments rich in reading materials; and in families that valued reading, both independently and together. One participant explicitly stated that she grew up in a "culture of reading." Individuals must remember that literacy itself isn't just "being able to read." Instead, it is creating a culture where words are valued, whether those words be in written form or in other forms (such as audiobooks or storytelling). Not all of the unschoolers in this study read early or well right away, but most reported being read to or exposed to books in many forms. Reading aloud in unschooling families did not end when a child entered adolescence. Many participants recalled being read to even as older teens. Interest in reading and the written word came from one's individual intrinsic motivation and one's overall environment; and not from book clubs, book counts, or extrinsic rewards for completion of books. Book choice is also something to discuss. Participants in this study did report that one of the biggest benefits of reading within an unschooling environment was the choice they had in books and reading materials. Books were rarely censored, and unschoolers were free to choose books they wanted to read/had an interest in, regardless of reading level. Many participants shared that they frequently read books above their level as a personal challenge. As stated in previous studies (Gray and Riley, 2013; Riley, 2015), one of the biggest benefits of unschooling is reported as autonomy and choice; and book choice is an important part of the intellectual freedom unschoolers consistently report.

Second Language Learning

In Chapter 2, we learned that cultural transmission occurs without formal teaching, and is a way of learning and passing on information through familial or cultural norms (Reber, 1995). Cultural transmission is also an important aspect of the unschooling process, especially when it comes to second language learning. Some unschooled families travel a significant amount, and so second language acquisition comes from being immersed within a new language and culture. Other times, a parent or grandparent speaks a second language within the home, allowing the child or teen to hear and absorb that language. Still other unschoolers report falling in love with language in general, as shared by a participant in Riley's study of reading acquisition. She wrote: "My love of reading and language took me to graduate school for linguistics. I love orthographies (my personal specialty in the field), and can speak and read/write

Japanese fluently. I also dabble in Russian, Korean, Chinese, all the major Germanic languages, and Gaelic" (2018).

This is not to say that all unschoolers want or are motivated to study a language. Levin-Gutierrez (2015) explains that her youngest daughter is not at all intrinsically motivated to speak Spanish, even though Spanish is Levin-Gutierrez's first language. Guiterrez writes that as an unschooling parent, "I cannot impose the purpose of learning a second language to her. Instead, I keep trying to expose her to some of the language in the hopes she will find her own purpose (to learn Spanish). My expectations and purpose are clearly not the same as hers and this is respected" (2015, p. 38).

In the article "The Power of Unschooling: Why My Daughters Don't Go to School," Akilah Richards discusses how her daughters became interested in different language groups, sharing that one of her daughters would come across an image of a flag, then look online to find its related country. Richards' daughter then figured out that on Wikipedia, there is a section where a country's name is written in its native language. Seeing the name printed in its native language led to her to further exploring the languages themselves. That's when Richards' daughter started falling in love with languages (2016).

This path of looking at something of interest (the flag, in Richards' example above), seeing the country's name written in its national language, and then wanting to explore the language, is not uncommon to unschoolers. In unschooling, the study of one topic commonly leads to interest and study in another topic (Richards, 2016). This cross-disciplinary exploration is a frequent theme among unschoolers, which stands in sharp contrast to the clear demarcations between subjects which occurs in most conventional schools. As Currie-Knight expresses, "we wrongly think of things like math, history, and science as subjects. But they are not. They are ways of thinking" (2018). Currie-Knight then gives the example of math. In school, math is a subject that teachers tell students they must sit down and study. But in reality, Currie-Knight asserts, math is a skill. It is an ability needed in order to go about one's day. We need to be able to tell time to get to places we need to go to. We need to be able to count money and make change in order to purchase the food we need to live. We need to be able to cook and measure in order to feed ourselves. Math is everywhere, not just in text-books, and everything is interrelated. In unschooling, math is not just a separate subject you learn. Learning the skill of math comes naturally from life (2018). The process of unschooling takes a holistic approach to learning, and invites people to make connections between seemingly disparate topics, like numbers and cooking, or flags and foreign languages.

How Unschoolers Learn Math

In 2010, Peter Gray did an informal survey of how unschoolers learn math on his blog *Freedom to Learn*. Sixty-one readers responded to his call for participants, many explaining in depth how their children learned math in a self-directed way. Gray organized the personal stories he received into four categories, based on the motivation for math learning. These four categories were: playful math, instrumental math, didactic math, and college admissions math. Playful math was defined as math "used for no other purpose than the sheer fun and beauty of it. Playful math involves the discovery or production of patterns in numbers" (Gray, 2010). Most young children will naturally begin to understand that numbers come in a fixed sequence (think basic counting), and that there is a pattern to that counting. For example, one reader of Gray's blog submitted a story about her son, almost five, who learned counting through connect the dot activities. Another learned addition of 2 and 3 numbers by noticing the patterns on his Lego bricks.

Instrumental math was defined, in Gray's informal study, as math naturally learned in everyday life (2010). For example, many parents expressed that their children learned the basic math skills of addition, subtraction, multiplication, division, and percentages just by handling money or cooking. In baking for example, fractions are used frequently, and in some recipes, recipes need to be converted from teaspoons to milliliters and ounces to grams. Games like Uno, Monopoly, and Chess utilize both math and strategy. Music was also referred to as a huge catalyst for inadvertently practicing math skills. As one parent shared, "Playing the piano….my daughter was encountering fractions – half notes, quarter notes, eighth notes, sixteenth notes, all in musical notation" (2010).

Didactic math was defined as "math as it is taught by expert educators." Gray (2010) notes that many unschooled parents feel the need to teach math in a semi-formal way, by using workbooks and worksheets. However, over time, parents change their minds and stop the direct instruction, noticing that their children seek the math they need on their own. One commenter on Gray's blog shared that a friend's son had no formal math training, but at fourteen-years-old decided that he would like to take algebra at a local community college. He then purchased a basic math textbook and taught himself all he needed to know in less than a month (2010), supplementing textbook work with Kahn Academy videos.

The last category Gray used was "College Admissions Math" (2010). This is math needed for things like the Scholastic Aptitude Test (SAT), the ACT, or the GRE (Graduate Record Exam). Some unschooled students seek tutoring themselves for these aptitude tests, but others use the skills they learned as self-directed learners to figure out the math they need to know to pass the test. These self-directed skills include knowing where to go to get the information they need and utilizing self-obtained prep books or tutors. Also, most unschoolers inherently know that learning things that are considered difficult by the outside world really isn't that challenging if you put enough effort and time into them. Some parents, like Lainie Liberti, are not worried about their children learning didactic or college admissions math at the present time. As she asserts:

> As an unschooling parent, I am concerned with my son's interests now. If my son becomes interested in something that requires specific knowledge as a foundation, then I will get him the support to learn what he needs, now. I can't worry about what he may or may not be interested in the future, nor frankly is that my responsibility as an unschooling parent…I can only provide for his needs now, based on his interests. This empowers my son and puts the accountability on him, with the responsibility to communicate his needs. (2012)

History and Science Learning in Unschoolers

Most unschoolers take an interest-based approach to history, unlike in school, where it is generally studied using a chronological approach. As Currie-Knight expresses, "What is history except the ability to tell a story about how something has progressed over time?" (2018). When unschoolers visit a place, they learn about the history associated with that spot. When they see a movie or television show about a particular period of time, they may want to dig deeper to learn more about that moment. When someone famous catches an unschooler's interest, they may learn about the year or period that person was born in, and what was going on at that time (Concillo, 2020). History, for unschoolers, is usually "living history," and is made alive through trips to historic houses, places, museums, and reenactments. Music, dance, maps, websites, and newspapers are also always a starting point for further study of different cultures and customs.

Unschoolers and Science

Learning science is all about exploration and discovery, something unschoolers know a lot about. Most unschoolers spend a large majority of their days outside or in their neighborhood, exploring and asking questions about the world. In Ben Hewitt's book *Home Grown: Adventures in Parenting Off the Beaten Path, Unschooling, and Reconnecting with the Natural World*, Hewitt tells stories of his sons building wooden trucks with moveable parts, constructing forts that are weather resistant, feeding their livestock, and collecting edible plants and mushrooms. For those unschooling in the city, resources are unlimited. As Kerry McDonald states in Matthew Hennessey's article about home learning in the city "We use the city as our primary learning tool, taking advantage of all its offerings, including classes, museums, libraries, cultural events, and fascinating neighbors - including a Tufts University biology professor who brings home snails and mollusks for the kids" (2015).

In a study of unschooled adults, twenty-nine percent chose STEM (science, technology, engineering, or math)-based careers (Gray and Riley, 2015), and a majority chose those careers based on childhood interests and experiences. The Maker Movement, a movement dedicated to active STEM learning within a group environment, has reinvigorated unschoolers' motivations to experiment with and make older inventions better, as well as to create new innovations within collaborative spaces (Taylor, 2020). Unschoolers tend to live and breathe science on a daily basis, no curriculum needed.

Gaps in Learning

A common question people have about unschooling is "Won't unschoolers have gaps in learning if they are only learning about what they are interested in?" (Fuglei, 2015). This question most likely stems from the only quantitative study that reviewed the academic success of homeschooled students, conducted by Martin-Chang, Gould, and Meuse in 2011. These researchers compared standardized test scores of homeschooled students with a demographically similar group of traditionally schooled students between the ages of 5–10. At one point in the study, they interviewed the mothers of those students who identified themselves as homeschooled and found that 12 of them described their homeschool method as unstructured or relaxed homeschooling (9 of the mothers used the term unschooling within their description). Noting this, Martin-Chang, Gould, and Meuse separated these 12 children from other homeschoolers and treated them as a separate group. The main finding of the study was that those who identified as homeschoolers significantly outperformed the traditionally schooled students on all academic tests. The researchers then decided to compare the scores of the unstructured homeschoolers with those of the other two groups and found those scores to be lower than those of the structured homeschoolers and the traditionally schooled students. This isolated study is many times referred to by others as proof that unschoolers tend to have poorer academic outcomes than traditionally schooled or unschooled students (Fuglei, 2015), and is taken as a major academic criticism of unschooling.

Academics that study homeschooling and unschooling, as well as unschoolers themselves tend to be unsurprised, but critical, of the finding (Gaither, 2018; Gray and Riley, 2015). In Riley's study, focused on unschoolers reading, a participant noted:

> ...I have read something about unschoolers (at 8, 9, or 10) not testing very well when you compare them to kids at school....with the relaxed approach, so many of my friends really became academic at 12 or 14, and they are doing well in community college as teens, like I am. Of course people who do not 'do school' will not do well on things that measure how well you 'do school' at a young age. (2018)

Of course, traditionally schooled students and homeschooled students that are used to yearly standardized academic testing will do better on standardized tests. This is why so much time and energy is spent on test preparation in traditional schools. Also, the one test that the 12 students categorized as "unstructured homeschooled students" did the poorest on was in reading. However, studies on unschoolers and reading (Gray, 2010; Pattison, 2016; Riley, 2018) have revealed that some unschooled children don't learn to read until after age 7, but then become highly proficient readers quickly (Gray and Riley, 2015). We don't know the exact ages of the unstructured homeschoolers in Martin-Chang et al.'s

(2011) study, but it would be interesting to see if they were under the age of 7. Also, it is essential to note that the comparison of data focused on "unstructured homeschoolers" was done as an afterthought, during a time in which the study was already in progress. The initial intention of the study was to compare homeschoolers with traditionally schooled students.

Taking full consideration of all data, however, the short answer is yes. Just as schooled students have gaps in learning, unschooled students will too. For example, less than one percent of American adults are proficient in a language that they studied for an extended period of time within a U.S. classroom (Friedman, 2015), and American students consistently score poorly on international assessments focused on math (Johnson, 2019), despite being formally taught math for 180 days or more during the school year. In addition, two out of three traditionally schooled children did not meet U.S. standards for reading proficiency set by the National Assessment of Educational Progress, leading current U.S. Educational Secretary Betsy Devos to declare "a student achievement crisis" in American schools (Green and Goldstein, 2019).

As Idzie Desmaris, an adult unschooler reflects:

> In my teens I used to worry that I had "gaps" when compared to schooled peers, but the older I got the more apparent it became just how different everyone's skills were. I realized that I was better at some things than some people, and other people were better at other things. I knew more about some subjects, and less about others, just like all of my friends, whether schooled, homeschooled, or unschooled. (2020)

Unschooling creates a different environment for learning, one that is difficult to study in a traditional way. However, it is clear that unschoolers learn, and learn well, with a focus on the subjects and topics they are most interested in. These childhood interests, in a large majority of unschoolers, turn into financially successful careers as unschoolers proceed into adulthood (Gray and Riley, 2015). Although unschooled learning may not be developmentally linear, it is efficient, exploratory, imaginative, and self-determined, all positive attributes that stakeholders and researchers within the world of education should take note of.

References

Camera, L. (2019, October 30). Across the board, scores drop in math and reading for U.S. students. U.S. *News and World Report*. https://www.usnews.com/news/education-news/articles/2019-10-30/across-the-board-scores-drop-in-math-.

Concillo, J. (2020). *You can't escape the past: Unschooling history*. https://unschoolrules.com/unschooling-history/.

Csoli, K. (2013). Natural learning and learning disabilities: What I've learned as the parent of a 2 year old. *Journal of Unschooling and Alternative Learning, 7*, 92–104.

Currie-Knight, K. (2018, September 21). Ways of thinking, not school subjects. *Tipping Points*. https://www.self-directed.org/tp/ways-of-thinking/.

Desmaris, I. (2020). Do unschoolers have gaps in their education. *HomeSchool-Life Blog*. https://homeschoollifemag.com/blog/do-unschoolers-have-gaps-in-their-education.

Evans, M. D. R., Kelley, J., Sikora, J., & Treiman, D. J. (2010). Family scholarly culture and educational success: Books and schooling in 27 nations. *Research in Social Stratification and Mobility, 28*, 171–197.

Friedman, A. (2015, May 10). America's lacking language skills. *The Atlantic*. https://www.theatlantic.com/education/archive/2015/05/filling-americas-language-education-potholes/392876/.

Fuglei, M. (2015, January 21). *Unschooling: Inspirational learning method or educational neglect?* https://education.cu-portland.edu/blog/classroom-resources/unschooling/.

Gaither, M. (2018). *Homeschool: An American history*. New York: Palgrave Macmillan.

Gray, P. (2010, February 21). *Children teach themselves to read*. https://www.psychologytoday.com/blog/freedom-learn/201002/children-teach-themselves-read.

Gray, P., & Riley, G. (2013). The challenges and benefits of unschooling according to 232 families who have chosen that route. *Journal of Unschooling and Alternative Learning, 7*, 1–27.

Gray, P., & Riley, G. (2015). Grown unschoolers' evaluations of their unschooling experience: Report I on a survey of 75 unschooled adults. *Other Education, 4*(2), 8–32.

Green, E. L., & Goldsten, D. (2019, December 5). Reading scores on national exam decline in half the states. *The New York Times*. https://www.nytimes.com/2019/10/30/us/reading-scores-national-exam.html.

Hauseman, D. C. (2011). "Nerdy know it all's and "Paranoid Parents": Images of alternative learning in films and television programs. *Journal of Unschooling and Alternative Learning, 5*, 1–17.

Hennessey, M. (2015, Summer). Homeschooling in the city: Frustrated with public schools, middle class urbanites embrace an educational movement. *City Journal*. https://www.city-journal.org/html/homeschooling-city-13742.html.

Hewitt, B. (2014). *Home Grown: Adventures in parenting off the beaten path, unschooling, and reconnecting with the natural world*. Boston: Roost Books.

Johnson, S. (2019, December 3). *U.S. math scores remain flat on international test of 15 year olds*. https://edsource.org/2019/u-s-math-scores-remain-flat-on-international-test-of-15-year-olds/620711.

Johnson, V. (2015). The power of the read aloud in the age of the common core. *The Open Communication Journal, 9*, 34–38.

Lancy, D. F., Bock, J., & Gaskins, S. (2014). *The anthropology of learning in childhood*. Lantham, MD: AltaMira Press.

Levin-Gutierrez, M. (2015). Motivation: Kept alive through unschooling. *Journal of Unschooling and Alternative Learning, 9*, 32–41.

Liberti, L. (2012). Unschooling: Is teaching higher level mathematics important. *Raising Miro on the Road of Life*. http://www.raisingmiro.com/2012/10/08/unschooling-math-beyond-the-basics/.

Martin-Chang, S., Gould, O. N., & Meuse, R. E. (2011). The impact of schooling on academic achievement: Evidence from homeschooled and traditionally schooled students. *Canadian Journal of Behavioral Science, 43*, 195–202.

Pattison, H. (2016). *Rethinking learning to read*. Shrewsbury, UK: Educational Heretics Press.

Reber, A. S. (Ed.). (1995). *The Penguin dictionary of psychology* (2nd ed.). New York: Penguin.

Richards, A. (2016, December 23). *The power of unschooling: Why my daughter's don't go to school*. http://www.ravishly.com/2016/08/26/power-unschooling-why-my-daughters-dont-go-school.

Riley, G. (2015). Differences in competence, autonomy, and relatedness between home educated and traditionally educated young adults. *International Social Science Review*, 90(2), 1–27.

Riley, G. (2018). Exploring unschoolers' experiences in learning to read: How reading happens within the self-directed learning environment. *Journal of Unschooling and Alternative Learning*, 12(24), 1–33.

Riley, G., & Gray, P. (2015). Grown unschoolers' experiences with higher education and employment: Report II on a survey of 75 unschooled adults. *Other Education, 4*(2), 33–53.

Taylor, K. (2020). *Parts and crafts*. https://www.partsandcrafts.org/about-us/theory-and-philospphy/free-schools-and-makerspaces/.

Wheatley, K. (2013). How unschoolers can help to end traditional reading instruction. *Journal of Unschooling and Alternative Learning, 7*, 1–28.

CHAPTER 8

The Challenges and Benefits of Unschooling

In Gray and Riley's 2013 qualitative study of 232 families who chose unschooling, questions were asked about the challenges and benefits of unschooling. Families most frequently identified challenges relating to feelings of social pressure or criticism regarding the decision to unschool by relatives, neighbors, and friends. There were also challenges related to the difficulty of one or both parents ridding themselves of their own culturally ingrained attitudes and beliefs toward school and learning. Additionally, parents identified practical issues pertaining to time, career responsibilities, and income considerations. Socialization was seen as a challenge, as were specific legal issues associated with unschooling.

Social Pressure, Criticism, and Unschooling

The most frequent challenge, noted by 43.5% of respondents, was that of feeling social pressure. These families reported negative judgments from family, friends, neighbors, and even strangers regarding their choice to unschool. As one parent expressed, "The biggest hurdle has been other people. It's difficult to find others who are encouraging, especially people who live nearby" (Gray and Riley, 2013). Unschooling families also felt a constant need to justify their choice to others. This constant negative judgment and criticism was perceived as exhausting and anxiety-provoking (Gray and Riley, 2013). In Rolstad's study of self-efficacy in

G. Riley, *Unschooling*, Palgrave Studies in Alternative Education,
https://doi.org/10.1007/978-3-030-49292-2_8

unschooling mothers, many expressed how debilitating this incessant criticism can be (2016). It is especially difficult when criticism comes from inside the family. As one unschooling parent shared within the Gray and Riley (2013) study, "We still have not told my husband's family that we are unschooling. We fear they would panic and feel the need to step in. We don't want that tension for ourselves or our children." Another parent said, "My parents are both public school teachers who don't understand our decision to unschool. They barrage our children constantly with curriculum-based questions. We regularly have conversations about the choice and their disagreement with it." Even when they were not receiving or responding to public or verbal criticism, unschooling parents ceaselessly seem to work through imagined dialogue with critics (O'Hare and Coyne, 2019), both internally and through blogs or social media postings. Doing something that is perceived as countercultural always comes with difficulties, and so many individuals have preconceived ideas about what schooling and education should look like. Sharing one's opinions and outright disagreement can be hurtful for both the unschooling family and the children and teens involved.

Deschooling the Parents

Almost forty-two percent of respondents identified having culturally ingrained thoughts regarding teaching, schooling, and education as a challenge when pursuing unschooling. As one family in the Gray and Riley (2013) study said, "Our biggest challenge is to let her be, since both my husband and I thrived in public school, with the traditional sit, be quiet, and learn curriculum." Another family stated that the biggest challenge was the "unschooling of my husband and myself. We have had to do a lot of work on ourselves to be open to this. My son instinctively knows how to do this. We have had to unlearn a lot" (Gray and Riley, 2013). Karin Siakkos, in Una Hunderi's book *Born Free*, states that parental deschooling is difficult, as parents "have lost faith in their own abilities. They have been raised by the school system believing that they should always wait for instructions….that they are not good enough, that they don't know enough" (2019, n.p.). School has become an institution and a culture we follow and put our trust in, sometimes without thinking that there are other ways to live and educate.

Numerous parents feel that they are unequipped to educate their child without an advanced degree in education, believing that they need years of specialized training before they can effectively teach. This leads many people to doubt their own abilities as facilitators of learning and skill models. Most parents also live within a community where a large majority of children aged 5 through 18 attend school, making the school structure always prevalent in everyday life. As a parent in Gray and Riley's study shared, "Most people are stuck in the school paradigm and feel like it really is necessary for kids to go to school in order to be successful adults" (2013). Every time the school bus arrives for the neighbors' children, doubts creep up. When school vacation is over and there are no children outside at 10 a.m., parents question their choice. Each time a child is asked at the grocery store "what grade are you in?" or "what school do you go to?", unschooling parents cringe, and children occasionally won't know what to say. Unschooling creates a different paradigm for learning, one that is sometimes difficult to explain to outsiders.

Gray and Riley (2013) also saw a link between social pressure and culturally ingrained thoughts about learning and teaching. For example, other's criticisms and comments regarding the need for children to be in school "would sometimes reawaken old, socially normative ways of thinking and raise again the fears that unschooling parents thought they had overcome, even when they could see that unschooling was working very well for their children" (Gray and Riley, 2013, p. 12). These thoughts and fears sometimes led parents to a more direct instruction style of teaching that went against unschooling core philosophy and didn't work for their children. This, in turn, would sometimes cause parent/child friction as well as family tension, and an increase in the primary parent's stress levels (Rolstad, 2016). Then they would quickly go back to unschooling. As one family shared, "We have done a little homeschooling and were met with a lot of resistance from my son. He has always wanted to do things on his own and in his own way. Unschooling was a much better fit for our family" (Gray and Riley, 2013).

A few parents in the Gray and Riley study suffered from cognitive dissonance around unschooling because they truly believed in the power and mission of public schools. Choosing a path that is right for a particular family or an individual child does not automatically mean a parent disagrees with or is against other paths. In fact, one can be a huge supporter of public schools but still choose to unschool their child. As one participant wrote:

> My biggest personal challenge with this choice is my own beliefs about democracy....I long believed public schools are necessary and important, and have always supported them. However, I also believe in every family's right to raise their children without school and however they want. I realize that we are blessed in our ability to keep (our daughter) out of school, and we have made sacrifices in order to do so. I also know not every parent is able to provide their children with appropriate resources and support to find their way in the world without the benefit of public schooling. I feel conflicted when I discuss our choice with my public-school teacher friends, and when I think about what I truly believe about society and education. (2013)

On a personal note, I, the author, feel constant dissonance regarding my positions on both public schooling and unschooling. Although my research life revolves around unschooling and self-directed learning, and I personally have unschooled my own child, I spend a majority of my time every day working to make public education better. I am a professor of teacher education and coordinate a program that certifies adolescent special educators to teach in the largest school system in the United States. I believe deeply in my teacher candidates and their power to change public schools for the better. I see how much they care for their students, and how much time they devote to making their students' lives better. I love and respect each and every one of my teacher candidates, and genuinely honor their work. When I visit public schools, I see firsthand the dedication administrators, teachers, and staff have with regard to their schools and the students they serve. I live my life shuffling between two worlds, seeing the pros and cons of each. It gives me great perspective, but it is still sometimes taxing. Most of those who support unschooling are not against public schools, teachers, or formal systems of learning. Instead, we see the benefits of self-directed, intrinsically motivated learning and want to share those benefits with the world (or just with our individual children).

Time, Career, and Income Effects

Forty-five families within the study mentioned limits in time, career, and income as a challenge inherent in unschooling (Gray and Riley, 2013). Unschooling parents spend a lot of time with their children. Although they are not directly instructing their children, they are there as a resource, facilitator, and guide. They commonly drive their children to and from different activities and are involved in the scheduling of those activities. Some individuals send children to school primarily so they can work. Unschooling families choose to be home with their children so they can learn. The time spent with their children does affect the overall time they are able to spend working for income and engaging in self-care, but instead, they are providing an autonomous supportive environment for their child or children. As one parent in the Gray and Riley study stated "We scrimped a little on one income, but no amount of money could have recompensed me for the years we spent learning together" (2013). Other parents have chosen to quit jobs and start their own businesses so that they can work from home and unschool. Another parent expressed that, out of necessity, they had to rethink what self-care was in the context of the life stage they were in (2013). If self-care usually happened outside the home (i.e., going to a nail salon, or getting a massage), how could some of those activities shift or be replaced with things that can be done within the home?

It is crucial to consider that not all unschooling families include a stay at home parent or even two parents. Some unschooling families are led by single parents, and other families have working parents who take different shifts so one person can be with the child(ren) unschooling. For example, a single parent in Gray and Riley's study worked as a nanny and had her daughter come with her (2013). When I unschooled my son as a single mother, I took on work as an adjunct professor and taught online at numerous colleges for income so that I could be home for a few hours during the workday. Still other families utilize grandparents, unschooling cooperatives, and other forms of child care to be able to unschool their children. Unschooling parents sacrifice a lot to make things work, even in the most complicated of circumstances.

Chase and Morrison (2018) bring up the issue of the challenge of lack of cultural capital in their article focusing on multicultural education and unschooling. They state that most unschooling families must possess some cultural capital, or socioeconomic status, in order to feel prepared enough to embrace the unschooling philosophy. This is why traditional families that consider themselves middle or upper class are not as persecuted for unschooling when compared to more untraditional or unmarried parent counterparts. If parents do instead embrace the philosophy without cultural capital, they risk additional hardships and marginalization from society. First, from their social standing in society, and second, from their untraditional educational choice. Despite the increased marginalization, there are many single parents and those within marginalized groups taking the leap and unschooling their children happily. Unschooling is no longer the domain of white, two-parent families.

The "gig economy" we see in this new decade has also increased the number of parents that can unschool their children. These independent contractors can balance work and home life and still utilize their talents and education in a way that works for them. This new way of working has much in common with unschooling, as it focuses on flexibility, autonomy, and freedom (McDonald, 2018). Many unschooling parents own their own businesses, babysit, drive ride-sharing automobiles, or teach classes as freelancers at schools, colleges, community centers, libraries and local music, dance, or yoga studios. Others coach or tutor, and bring their child with them to work.

The advent of the internet has also provided many with full-time jobs with reputable companies or nonprofit organizations that can be done remotely. These jobs include comprehensive benefits and allow a parent to receive full salary and health insurance while still being able to work primarily at home. While the parent is working, the child can be working too on their own reading, writing, music, or individual, self-directed projects. Meal and break times can be utilized strategically, so the child can ask for support, resources, or assistance when needed. There are many ways to make unschooling work.

Finding Friends

Forty-five families mentioned finding friends as a challenge inherent in unschooling (Gray and Riley, 2013). This challenge referred not just to children or teens finding friends, but also unschooling parents being able to find friends. The schooled world provides an instant social arena for children and parents alike. Children enter classrooms of same-aged peers, and parents gain an instant social connection when associating with parents of their children's classmates. In an unschooling environment, both parent and child or teen have to actively seek friendships, and it can be difficult finding people who share a similar educational philosophy or have common interests. As an example, one respondent to the Gray and Riley (2013) study shared:

> We do not fit in everywhere, that is for sure. We have had friends lost because parents have been unable to deal with the freedom we live in - their kids come home and want to know why they have to do this and so when our child does not, and so on. It is often like feeling our way down a dark hallway, but the rewards in lifestyle and relationship has been worth it.

Another wrote:

> It can be sort of a lonely road in the sense that, although there is a great online unschooling community, there aren't too many people in real life who parent this way and who share my educational philosophies. My husband and I try to parent and live according to our ideas, but it is hard not having anyone in real life that models this way for us. Sometimes I wish we had a mentor, or even just a good friend who shared our values that we could talk to and hang out with.

Unschooling groups and conferences have been helpful for children and teens who want and need to form bonds with other unschoolers. Specifically, Not Back to School Camp has been a particularly supportive place for older unschoolers. Not Back to School Camp, founded by writer and unschooling advocate Grace Llewellen, is a place where teens aged 13–18 can connect with other unschoolers in a transformative way. It is a loving, accepting, growth affirming gathering of those who have been alternatively educated (Not Back to School Camp, 2020) and was noted by many grown unschoolers (Gray and Riley, 2015), as a place where they felt the most social support as adolescents.

Locally, unschooling groups provide activities, information, and encouragement for unschooling families. Some unschooling groups also have associated unschooling cooperatives, where families get together, rent a space, and offer different classes on topics their children are interested in. Regional unschooling conferences are also spaces where parents can attend sessions around topics related to unschooling, and children and teens can "find their tribe," socialize with, and play or bond with other unschoolers (Laricchia, 2018).

Legal Issues

Legal issues or problems deriving from laws or district regulations that make unschooling hard to practice were mentioned by fifteen families as a challenge to unschooling (Gray and Riley, 2013). One parent shared,

"Society and government want to quantify learning…This is offensive and is a big challenge. Currently, in our state, I have to give my child a standardized test once a year…I worry about this affecting my commitment to unschooling" (Gray and Riley, 2013). In the United States, each state has its own educational regulations centered around homeschooling, and each district also has specific expectations regarding reporting and testing. Meeting these expectations of assessment and specific subject-based learning may be difficult in an unschooling environment, leading to issues with the state, district, and sometimes, reporting to local child protection agencies under the umbrella of "educational neglect." These factors can create fear in both those families who have been unschooling for a long time, as well as in new unschoolers.

Another fear is being arrested by authorities for unschooling, which is what happened to the Spell family of Leon County, Florida. The Spells were charged in 2013 with 10 misdemeanors for "failing to educate their eight children" after a family member complained to authorities. The charges against them included contributing to the delinquency of a minor and violations of compulsory attendance (Hatter, 2013). Numerous other arrests have followed, mostly due to state authorities' and overall societal lack of understanding regarding homeschooling and unschooling (Beasley, 2019; Buelher, 2017; Larkin, 2018). The Home School Legal Defense Association asserts that recent arrests illustrate demonization of "the smallest and least understood part of the homeschooling movement" (Slatter, 2010).

One parent in the Gray and Riley (2013) study stated that her family and friends commonly threatened that she was abusing her kids by unschooling; "However, theirs are in juvenile or out on the streets at all hours. My oldest is working on taking college level classes at 15." Another was frustrated by the ignorance of psychologists, social workers, lawyers, and court officials regarding the basic tenets of unschooling. She stated "I am literally fighting the system. It is exhausting." Liberto (2016) recommends that state and local districts and regulators gain increased understanding regarding both the unschooling movement and the value of student-led, internally motivated learning.

The Benefits of Unschooling

Within the Gray and Riley (2013) study, the benefits of unschooling seemed to outweigh the challenges. Benefits described centered on advantages for not only the child or children unschooling, but also for the parents and the family structure as a whole. Specific benefits mentioned included increased student learning and motivation, added family closeness, and improved family freedom of schedule. Other benefits were also written about by the participants of this study.

Increased Student Learning

Increased student learning was mentioned by 57.3% of respondents. These parents reported an increase in curiosity and intrinsic motivation to learn, as well as strengthened practical learning skills. Levin-Gutierrez (2015) agrees, stating that "unschooling provides a system where individual interests are nurtured and therefore intrinsic motivation is maintained" (p. 39). As one parent in the Gray and Riley (2013) study said of her daughter "watching her engaged in the things that interest her has been a lesson in and of itself...she can work for hours on something that is meaningful to her." Another parent mentioned "enthusiasm for learning" has been the best part of the unschooling experience, and wrote "I am constantly amazed at the questions my daughter asks and how her learning seems to evolve naturally in her own time" (Gray and Riley, 2013). Still another shares "Our kids learn all the time, instead of being trained to learn one subject at a time, in 50 min increments bookended by bells" (Gray and Riley, 2013).

When learning is not pressured or forced in any way, amazing things can occur. For example, a parent described her children's learning within an unschooled environment in this way:

> I think it's awesome when my eight-year-old comes up to me and asks if we can look up things about World War I and II because he wants to know the difference between the two; or when the boys spend a Saturday setting up a science experiment just for the fun of it. Their learning is intrinsic so it means something; rather than them being spoon-fed things that mean nothing to them....We never know where the day is going to lead us. Just two nights ago we were discussing states of matter and ended blowing up balloons using vinegar and baking soda. I just don't think these things

> would happen if we were on someone else's schedule and were being told what my boys had to learn and when they were allowed to learn it.

In schools, teachers must get through a specific amount of curriculum in a specific time. This means learning does not happen naturally, and students are exposed to material they may not be interested in and/or may not be developmentally or academically ready for. As Arnall says in her book, *Unschooling to University*, "Learning is not always an outcome of teaching. Learning happens when the learner merges new information with previously held information. It involves the important brain functions of memory, perception, and concept formation. These tasks are all under the learner's control, not the teacher's" (2018, p. 161).

Social-Emotional Benefits

Fifty-two point one percent of respondents mentioned the social and emotional benefits of unschooling. Specifically, they said that their children were happier, more playful, less stressed, and more confident within an unschooling environment. Many parents whose children had social-emotional issues or special education classifications at school saw those issues disappear once the children felt safe within the unschooling realm. As one parent shared "Unschooling saved both my kids' self-esteem for different reasons" (Gray and Riley, 2013). Dr. Peter Gray, in an informal study of students with ADHD who had been homeschooled, unschooled, or freeschooled, found that most children who had been medicated for ADHD while in conventional school were taken off their medications once they were removed from the traditional school environment. Those who never attended conventional school were never medicated. Gray surmises that this is because a majority of diagnostic symptoms attributed to ADHD, such as "making careless mistakes in schoolwork" or "not following through on instructions or assignments" are school-based, and those diagnostic symptoms are irrelevant when one isn't enrolled in school. He also established that taking a child out of school and doing school at home, or replicating the school environment wouldn't work, making unschooling or self-directed learning an ideal form of education for a child or teen with ADHD. Other findings included an increase in positive behavior, mood, and learning once a child stopped conventional schooling, and a greater ability to cope with the symptoms of ADHD once a child was released from school-based expectations. A student with

ADHD's ability to hyper focus was also seen as a benefit within a self-directed learning environment, as students could then take that hyper focus and make it work for them in exploring their passions and interests. Although small and not peer reviewed, this is an essential study, as it is the only one that a researcher has conducted to date concerning the outcomes of students diagnosed with ADHD outside the traditional school environment (Gray, 2010).

Many parents were also surprised or happy about the social benefits they observed while unschooling their children. One of the first questions people ask about homeschooling or unschooling tends to be "But how do they make friends?" Unschoolers make friends just like everyone else…by interacting with those who have common interests or values, or who happen to be at the same place during the same time. Although "social awkwardness" tends to be a stereotype about those who homeschool or unschool (Desmarais, 2010), those involved in the actual practice felt the opposite. They witnessed how joyfully their children or teens approached other people, regardless of their age, social status, gender identification, ability orientation, or race. For example, one unschooling parent mentioned how gratified they felt to see their child "speak intelligently with adults about a wide range of subjects" (Gray and Riley, 2013) and play so kindly with other children in the neighborhood. Another parent reported that their children "are happy to include everyone and don't have issues with gender, age, or trying to change to fit in that we see in their schooled friends" (Gray and Riley, 2013). Parents saw the benefits of socializing in real-world situations, and not just in classroom situations limited by age or grade. One respondent shared that, by unschooling, her child is "exposed to a variety of situations out in public that many other children her age never encounter and handles them well" (Gray and Riley, 2013). Another parent mentioned the close relationships their children have with not only other children, but also the adults around them. Their neighbors, the librarian at their local library, the bank teller, an older woman at church, and a favorite grocery store clerk have all become adored friends (Gray and Riley, 2013).

Family Relationships

Fifty-seven percent of families in the Gray and Riley (2013) study mentioned family closeness as a benefit of unschooling. When a parent is with a child or teen for so many hours per day, it is hard not to get along.

This family closeness also extends to siblings and grandparents as well. One parent stated, "I love that my kids are not separated from each other. They have very close and sweet bonds" (Gray and Riley, 2013). Another parent expressed the increased family closeness was especially true for her husband, who works an untraditional schedule. She reflects:

> I'm so happy that both me and my husband know our children so well, and that I don't have to catch my husband up with what is going on at the end of the day. We are true partners in parenting. This may not seem like it is directly related to unschooling, but I think it is. For us, unschooling is a whole lifestyle, where we spend lots of time together as a family, learning together and loving each other. Being close to our kids, both emotionally and physically, is important to us. I imagine that closeness will continue through the infamous teen years right into adulthood if we do it right. That's really important to me.

However, in *Born Free*, (Hunderi, 2019) Dr. Peter Gray expresses that children and teens enjoy the freedom from family that unschooling may provide. He states that it is natural to see children, and particularly older children, want to spend time away from their families. They are curious about other people's lives and their ideas. Unschooling also provides the freedom to spend time with others (neighbors, friends, and coworkers) who are not family, in an extended way. As Gray says, "I believe some people overemphasize the value of family closeness and family connectedness, and underemphasize the value of the child moving out from the family, making other connections and gaining an understanding of the diversity of society" (Hunderi, 2019, n.p.).

One criticism of unschooling tends to be centered on how much time unschoolers spend with their families and in their neighborhoods, instead of being exposed to the outside world. Although this criticism is not entirely valid, as many unschoolers choose to travel away from their families and communities and encounter new things quite often, Chase and Morrison (2018) agree that the more unschoolers are exposed to diversity, disadvantage, and social inequity, the better. This extended exposure to the world is essential for all, both schooled and unschooled, in order to develop into humans with vast multicultural knowledge, as well as a dedication to equality and openness of experience.

Family and Individual Freedom of Schedule

Over thirty-six percent of respondents mentioned family freedom of schedule as another benefit to unschooling. Unschooling families relished the fact that they didn't have to follow traditional school schedules, either daily or weekly, and could choose activities and travel whenever they wanted to. Some individuals traveled within their own town, others traveled far and wide, unencumbered by a school calendar. As one parent expressed, "We are so free. Free to set vacation schedules. Free to pick what we want to do" (Gray and Riley, 2013).

Although families mentioned several benefits of unschooling, they were also realistic in their view of the advantages of unschooling. They know that unschooling is not a cure-all, but have hope that it provides a change in the way individuals look at education, community, and schooling as a whole. They also do it because they know how it has changed their children. One participant expressed:

> Unschooling is not a panacea that prevents all unhappiness or difficulty; it's important not to oversimplify or romanticize this. Our daughters have had problems and struggles like all teenagers do in our society. They are extremely smart and well educated, but I think that would be true if they had gone to school. I think the biggest difference is that they know themselves better than we did at their age. They may be a little closer to their true path in life. That was certainly our hope, and if it turns out to be true, it's worth a lot. (Gray and Riley, 2013)

Although not included as a distinct benefit in Gray and Riley's (2013) study, the time and space to get to know oneself better is a distinct advantage to unschooling, especially during the adolescent years. Unschooling parents, on the whole, reported less instability during the teen years, and an increased sense of relatedness (Gray and Riley, 2013). Unschooled adults also report a strong bond with family (Gray and Riley, 2015), as well as unlimited time to explore ideas and interests (Gray and Riley, 2015; Jodah, 2017). They also find courage, based on their alternative educational backgrounds, to do things differently, and to become the innovators and creators of their own individual journeys through life (Gray, 2018; Jodah, 2017).

Eighteen-year-old musician Billie Eilish, now a five-time Grammy award winner, as well as her brother, producer and composer Finneas O'Connell, credits their lifetime of being homeschooled (and, in terms of the definitions used in this book, unschooled) to the success they experience today (Gillespie, 2020). As Eilish says, "I still learned everything. I just learned it from life" (Pitchfork, 2018). In a recent interview in Vogue, she also expressed, "I'm so glad I didn't go to school, because if I had, I would never have the life I have now" (Haskell, 2020).

In a 2014 conversation with Susan Borison, Eilish's brother Finneas O'Connell shared:

> Being homeschooled is all about self-discovery. It's something that I've really enjoyed and thrived under. I'm not at a high school where I have to base my self-worth off what other people think of me. I have to think, "What would I like to be doing? How would I like to be as a person?" I think that's an enormously positive thing.

Unschooling is not an easy route for any family to take. Much personal, social, and financial sacrifice is involved. Societal, legal, and sometimes familial dissent make the choice even more difficult. However, for most families, the benefits of unschooling far outweigh the challenges and risks. A love of learning is a huge benefit of unschooling. So is increased family closeness and the freedom families feel when they detach themselves from the traditional school calendar. For some, unschooling is deeply healing, and a way to escape school-based diagnoses and classifications that so often categorize a student for life. Although unschooling is not a cure-all, it is a legitimate path for learning that should be deeply respected.

References

Arnall, J. (2018). *Unschooling to university: Relationships matter most in a world crammed with content*. Calgary, AB: Professional Publishing.

Beasley, D. (2019, February 5). Mom arrested and booked for homeschooling. *Home School Legal Defense Association*. https://hslda.org/content/hs/state/ms/20190204-mom-arrested-and-booked-for-homeschooling.aspx.

Borison, S. (2014). Talking with Maggie Baird and Finneas O'Connell of Life Inside Out. *Your Teen*. https://yourteenmag.com/stuff-we-love/celebrity-interviews/talking-with-maggie-baird-and-finneas-oconnell.

Buelher, H. (2017, February 16). Was Buffalo mom jailed over homeschooling decision? *WKBW Buffalo*. https://www.wkbw.com/news/was-buffalo-mom-jailed-over-homeschooling-decision.

Chase, S. L., & Morrison, K. (2018). Implementation of multicultural education in unschooling and its potential. *International Journal of Multicultural Education, 20,* 39–59.

Desmarais, I. (2010, August 15). The myth of social awkwardness among homeschoolers and unschoolers. *I'm Unschooled. Yes, I Can Write.* http://yes-i-can-write.blogspot.com/2010/08/myth-of-social-awkwardness-among.html.

Gillespie. N. (2020, January 28). Sibling Grammy winners Billie Eilish and Finneas O'Connell praise homeschooling. *Reason Magazine.* https://reason.com/2020/01/28/sibling-grammy-winners-billie-eilish-and-finneas-oconnell-praise-homeschooling/?fbclid=IwAR1QU8a48Z_ExvNQyldcv9Fzjd98rPKWunb4qCsluP7SLWALJEGgsUlr2oE.

Gray, P. (2010). Experiences of ADHD labeled kids who leave typical schooling. Free to learn. *Psychology Today.* https://www.psychologytoday.com/us/blog/freedom-learn/201009/experiences-adhd-labeled-kids-who-leave-typical-schooling.

Gray, P. (2018). *How schools thwart our passions* [video]. YouTube. https://www.youtube.com/watch?v=coMXLy8RBIc.

Gray, P., & Riley, G. (2013). The challenges and benefits of unschooling, according to 232 families who have chosen that route. *The Journal of Unschooling and Alternative Learning, 7,* 1–27.

Gray, P., & Riley, G. (2015). Grown unschoolers' evaluations of their unschooling experience: Report I on a survey of 75 unschooled adults. *Other Education, 4*(2), 8–32.

Haskell, R. (2020, February 3). How Billie Eilish is reinventing pop stardom. *Vogue Magazine.* https://www.vogue.com/article/billie-eilish-cover-march-2020?fbclid=IwAR2Y46HJQXelbXYTjYsBaPcelgoPxlV9ZZlB6Sk8L4599GKM1RB8F I5ZN8.

Hatter, L. (2013, October 2). Parents arrested for not teaching their home-schooled children say they are innocent. *WFSU News.* https://news.wfsu.org/post/parents-arrested-not-teaching-their-home-schooled-children-say-theyre-innocent.

Hunderi, U. (2019). *Born free.* Oslo, Norway: Billedkunstnernes Vederlagsfond.

Jodah, M. (2017). Unschooling and how I became liberated: The teenage liberation handbook, quitting school, and getting a real life and education. *Journal of Unschooling and Alternative Learning, 11,* 1–7.

Laricchia, P. (2018). *The unschooling journey: A field guide.* Forever Curious Press.

Larkin, M. (2018, December 7). Homeschooling parent in Worcester was arrested in her home. Now she's suing. *WBUR.* https://www.wbur.org/edify/2018/12/07/josilyn-goodall-home-school-worcester-lawsuit.

Levin-Gutierrez, M. (2015). Motivation: Kept alive through unschooling. *Journal of Unschooling and Alternative Learning, 9,* 32–41.

Liberto, G. (2016). Child-led and interest-inspired learning, home education, learning differences and the impact of regulation. *Cogent Education, 3*, 1–10.

McDonald, K. (2018, July 16). How the gig economy empowers unschoolers. *Foundation for Economic Education*. https://fee.org/articles/how-the-gig-economy-empowers-unschoolers/.

Not Back to School Camp. (2020). https://www.nbtsc.org/.

O'Hare, A., & Coyne, J. (2019). Unschooling and the self: A dialogical analysis of unschooling blogs in Australia and New Zealand. *Culture & Psychology*. https://journals.sagepub.com/doi/abs/10.1177/1354067X19877914?journalCode=capa.

Pitchfork Media. (2018). *Billie Eilish rates being homeschooled, goth, and invisalign* [video]. YouTube. https://www.youtube.com/watch?time_continue=334&v=YavL_IVSGV4&feature=emb_title.

Rolstad, K. (2016). Factors influencing and limiting self-efficacy in unschooling mothers. *Journal of Unschooling and Alternative Learning, 10*, 49–81.

Slatter, I. (2010). Critique of 'unschooling' misses the point. *Home School Legal Defense Association*. https://hslda.org/content/docs/news/201005200.asp.

CHAPTER 9

Grown Unschooling Outcomes

Numerous researchers have done studies on the outcomes of adults who have been homeschooled. Ray (2017) notes a positive correlation between high academic achievement and the homeschooling population. Cogan (2010) reports that homeschooled students have higher ACT scores, grade point averages, and graduation rates as compared to traditionally schooled students. Montes (2015) confirms that homeschooled students are not at risk for socialization issues in the United States, although they were less likely to participate in school sports. Webb (2006) remarks that homeschooled students are often better socialized as compared to their schooled peers. Webb's study also concluded that home-educated adults who want to pursue higher education could do so with no evident barriers or prejudice, and that specific personality attributes of homeschooled adults are seen as beneficial to obtaining steady employment.

When taking into consideration democratic schooling outcomes, where students shape their day through being involved in their own personal interests and intrinsic motivations (Gray and Chanoff, 1986), positive outcomes were also seen. A large majority of the Sudbury Valley School alumni Gray and Chanoff surveyed reported having positive career experiences that matched their personal interests, and a preponderance of participants felt attending a democratic school was a benefit in terms of pursuing employment. In her Master's thesis, Miedima (2016) interviewed graduates of the Sands School, a democratic school in Britain,

G. Riley, *Unschooling*, Palgrave Studies in Alternative Education,
https://doi.org/10.1007/978-3-030-49292-2_9

and found that the alumni appreciated how the school shaped their moral character. Specifically, former students felt that their character was built by having the freedom to explore who they really were, having sole responsibility over their own lives, and growing up with the knowledge that there are always options and choices within every situation.

The only peer-reviewed research study on unschooled adult outcomes was a two-part study published in 2015 by Peter Gray and Gina Riley. This investigation had a sample size of 75 who had been unschooled for at least what have been their last two years of high school. A majority of participants were unschooled for many more years than two, and some had been unschooled throughout their entire school career.

The questionnaire Gray and Riley created asked about basic demographic information, the student's history of school, homeschool, or unschool, the reasoning for unschooling, who initiated the unschooling, the type of unschooling pursued, and any formal higher education participated in after unschooling. The study also asked about current and past employment, social life, and perceptions of the advantages and disadvantages of unschooling. Additionally, the investigators asked whether participants would consider unschooling their own children, if they decided to have any. Seventy-five participants met the criteria for the study, with a median age of 24 years (range 18–49 years). Seventy-seven percent of respondents were women, 16 respondents were men, and one participant identified as genderqueer. For purposes of comparison, Gray and Riley divided participants into three groups: those where were entirely unschooled, with no period of schooling or homeschooling; those who had no schooling or homeschooling beyond sixth grade; and those who been to school or were homeschooled beyond sixth grade. The groups were similar in terms of sample size and demographics (Gray and Riley, 2015; Riley and Gray, 2015).

Unschooled Adult's Perceptions of Socialization

Within the Gray and Riley (2013) study of unschooling families, parents generally reported their children being well socialized. Unschooled adults tended to agree, as 69% of participants reported their social life during their years of unschooling as good. As one participant explained, "I was a busy social child, and my sisters and I were enrolled in many evening and weekend activities. My social experiences as an unschooled youth are similar to the social experiences I have now – I seek out groups of people who have common values to myself who are interested in creating meaningful change" (Gray and Riley, 2015). Many stated that their local home or unschooling group was the main provider of social activities and a major source of friendships (53%). Forty-three percent stated that after-school activities provided a way to make friends. This included music, dance, sports, theater, and art classes, as well as church or religious group functions or clubs like Scouts or the youth development organization 4-H. Others made friends through work, family connections, or camp.

Twelve percent of respondents answered the socialization question in a way researchers coded as poor, and nineteen percent of respondents were coded as mixed. The majority of participants who gave responses coded as poor or mixed mentioned how the social stereotype of being homeschooled or unschooled negatively affected them. "I think it was a function of homeschooling and unschooling not being nearly as popular or accepted as it is now," one participant said (Gray and Riley, 2015). They also wrote of struggles finding friends with similar backgrounds or interests. A respondent wrote:

> It was a double whammy for my brother and me. We were homeschooled and lived on a boat. It didn't get much weirder than that. Homeschooling was still seen as something only religious nuts did, so I felt very awkward and out of place as a teenager. I wasn't into sports, so I didn't have that outlet either. I didn't truly feel comfortable around people my own age until probably my senior year of college, and I think that is only because my peers were adults, and I knew how to relate to that, if that makes sense. The upside to this experience is that it has made me very conscious of the social interaction my kids receive as unschoolers. (Gray and Riley, 2015)

Numerous participants, within the three coded categories, did mention that they wished they had more access to unschooled peers growing up. One participant shared, "The only thing I wish I had more of in my unschooling experience is a stronger community of unschooling teen peers." Another mentions "it would have been nicer to have a large base people doing a similar style of unschooling. During my years as a teenager, there weren't that many of us" (Gray and Riley, 2015). Some, however, indicated that they were introverts by nature, and were happy not to have forced social interactions.

Although the researchers didn't ask about age mixing, 68% of respondents mentioned that an advantage of unschooling was that they made friends and interacted with people of all different ages. Some went on to say that they felt socially advantaged because of this age mixing experience, and how similar it was to socialization that goes on in the real world after traditional schooling. One respondent shared, "Today, I continue to interact with people of all ages rather than seeking out people my own age. My friends range in age from teenagers to senior citizens 90+ years old" (Gray and Riley, 2015). Another participant expanded:

> How important is it, truly, to "meet other kids your age"? Just about the only place you may ever find yourself stuck around kids that are only your age is in school. Outside of that, at work, at the gym, at the coffee shop, and the neighborhood BBQ, at the bar, wherever you go you will most likely be interacting with people who are not all exactly your age. Unschooling gave me a leg up in the world by letting me interact with people of all ages. (Gray and Riley, 2015)

The Advantages of Unschooling According to Grown Unschoolers

The question about advantages of unschooling was answered enthusiastically by unschooled adults. Seventy-seven percent of participants responded with advantages researchers coded as time to pursue one's own interests. Seventy-five percent mentioned advantages coded as freedom and independence. These are similar categories, and when combined the investigators found that 95% talked about one of the two above. Sixty percent mentioned advantages coded as improved learning. As an example, one participant shared, "As a teenager, I cherished that unschooling led me to pursue my interests. It also opened up experiences that are extremely unlikely I would have had the opportunity for if I was schooled." Another wrote that "unschooling gave me the ability to process things deeply, to spend all day curled up with my journal imagining possibilities. It also gave me opportunity to become intimate with my interests" (Gray and Riley, 2015). Adult unschooler Astra Taylor remembers "In our house, the adults encouraged our interests, even those they found inscrutable, but did not instruct us or judge our progress. I spent months obsessed with making balloon animals" (2020).

In describing continuing effects in adulthood, 75% noted self-direction and/or self-motivation were significant benefits of unschooling. Others noted that unschooling gave them a high sense of responsibility and an interest in continued learning (many in this category stated it was because they were not "burnt out" by school). Some participants mentioned that unschooling created a smoother transition to adulthood, allowed them to avoid stressors associated with school, and gave them more time to spend with family. A few respondents wrote that unschooling gave them a "head start" when it came to beginning their higher education or career journey. As shared by the participants:

> As an adult, I see how strongly my independence and self-reliance were built during those years, especially with the traveling I did alone and then living away from my family working on farms. My curiosity and thirst for knowledge bloomed during my years unschooling, and I expect it will stay with me throughout my life. I'm not sure I would have been as confident asking questions or certain that what I was interested in was important if I hadn't been unschooled. I think the cultural assumption that we "learn" only when someone is teaching is quite detrimental to the entrepreneurial spirit of America and results in an uninterested, dispassionate citizenry. Unschooling kindled my passions and destroyed the concept that learning only occurs in structured environments. (Gray and Riley, 2015)

and

> The biggest advantage of unschooling was that it smoothed the transition to adulthood instead of all of a sudden being thrown out into the real world of college or career at age 18. I was able to begin exploring these things at a young age and at my own pace. At 15 I was able to take a college class, because I was interested, and see what college was like. At 16 I was able to start working a part time job, and slowly work more and more. I was able to enroll full time in college in what would have been my senior year of high school. I didn't have to wait…unschooling gave me the immediate benefit of time and space to explore my interests and ask myself questions such as "What kind of person am I?" and "Who do I want to be?", and then work to make those the same. (Gray and Riley, 2015)

The Disadvantages of Unschooling According to Grown Unschoolers

When it came to disadvantages, 37% of participants indicated "no disadvantage." One participant wrote "Honestly, I find no place where unschooling hindered me. Was being a teenager hard, and were there times of great struggle? Absolutely. But that would have been true no matter what I did for education" (Gray and Riley, 2015). A majority stated that the drawbacks of unschooling paled when compared to the advantages. The most frequent category of disadvantage was coded as others' opinions (28%). This was also the most frequently mentioned disadvantage in Gray and Riley's (2013) study of 232 unschooling families, and is a source of stress for unschooled children, teens, and parents alike. As one respondent shared, "I don't think there were really disadvantages that were specific to unschooling, unless you count the - what can only be called - persecution we experienced" (Gray and Riley, 2013). Another wrote:

> Growing up, I was discouraged by how many adults thought it was appropriate to tell me how I was probably never going to get into college, or be successful, or that I was being a difficult teenager and making my parents' lives harder. I see the lack of knowledge around unschooling as an option as a huge disadvantage, as well as the stigma against letting people be in charge of their own education. (Gray and Riley, 2015)

The next most common disadvantage coded was that of social isolation (21%), with unschooled adults noting that the difficulty of not having other unschoolers close by to play or hang out with. Also, schooled children tend to have different schedules than unschooled children, leading to increased feelings of loneliness. For example, a participant stated, "It was frustrating that the majority of my friends did go to school and thus weren't available most of the time, either due to their school hours or their heavy load of homework" (Gray and Riley, 2015). Only 8% mentioned any sort of learning deficit or gap they felt originated from unschooling, but most of the eight percent stated that they knew they could learn whatever they needed to know based on skills of self-direction and self-determination gained through unschooling (Gray and Riley, 2015).

There were three participants in the research who stated that the disadvantages of unschooling outweighed the advantages. All three of these individuals described their mothers having mental health issues and their fathers as uninvolved. These participants were not allowed to choose whether they wanted to be unschooled or whether they wanted to go to school. Two of them attributed the isolation somewhat to their parent's fundamental Christian beliefs. They all mentioned experiences they felt they were missing out on. As an example, one respondent dissatisfied with the unschooling experience shared:

> As a child, I was keenly aware of the many "normal" experiences, both positive and negative, that I was missing out on. My mother would talk fondly about her own high school experiences, her boyfriends and girlfriends, and band trips. I never learned how to play a musical instrument; as an unschooler, my parents would have to purchase lessons for me and they did not want to spend money on me. Missing out on these experiences, and sitting with the social isolation, was painful. (Gray and Riley, 2015)

Another disclosed:

> I did not have a choice about being unschooled, it was never discussed with me as something I could decide on. It was a lifestyle and very important to my mom so I never resisted it. She also repeatedly told me that "they would eat you alive" if I went to school. Even today, she talks about it as though she gave us a gift, even though I found it to be nothing but a disadvantage, at that time as well as today. (Gray and Riley, 2015)

It is important to look deeply at these cases, so that one can identify when unschooling can be a bad idea. Expanded accounts of these participant's experiences can be found within Gray and Riley's (2015) study in *Other Education*. Tara Westover's book *Educated* (2018) also tells the story of a less than ideal unschooling environment, and her book has many parallels to the stories we heard from the three participants that felt unschooling was a detriment to their lives. Unschooling is not something that works or is healthy for everyone, and is only one choice out of a variety of educational choices available to students.

Would Unschooled Adults Unschool Their Own Children?

When asked about whether participants would consider unschooling their own children, 67% of respondents stated that yes, they would unschool their own child unless the child expressed a clear preference for another form of education or unless circumstances prevented it. This number included the eight respondents of the study who already had children of school age and were unschooling them. Nineteen percent responded in a way investigators coded as maybe, stating that they would consider unschooling, but would look carefully at all possible options, including democratic schooling, free schooling, or progressive schooling. As one person shared, "Right now, I am really drawn toward democratic, non-coercive learning communities because of their emphasis on community building and the opportunity for peer to peer learning" (Gray and Riley, 2015). Five percent responded in a way the researchers coded as no, stating that they would not unschool their child or would be very unlikely to do so. Of these, two participants were among the three that felt that unschooling put them at a disadvantage in life (Gray and Riley, 2015).

Grown Unschoolers and Higher Education

In the second part of the study (Riley and Gray, 2015), the researchers asked about higher education and careers of those who have unschooled. Eighty-three percent of respondents had pursued some sort of higher education, including vocational school. Forty-four percent of participants had either completed a Bachelor's degree or were full-time undergraduate students at the time they responded to the questionnaire. Those in the always unschooled group were more likely to pursue a Bachelor's degree. A majority of participants who had not pursued any formal education felt that they did not need it. They were either confident that they could continue to learn what they needed to learn without formal schooling or that their current career choices did not demand further schooling. As one participant expressed:

> I have no plans to pursue formal higher education. I currently own my own freelance writing business. I have always loved writing and it was one of the many creative outlets I pursued as a homeschooler and an unschooler. I actually published my first book (a compilation of gospel arrangements for the banjo) during my teen years combining my musical talent with my writing ability. However, the most relevant trait I acquired as an unschooler is my love of learning new things. This makes it easy for me to "learn" new industries to serve an ever wider client base. My current career dovetails with my unschooling experience quite well. (Riley and Gray, 2015)

Getting into College

One question that is always asked of unschoolers pursuing higher education is "How did you get into college?" Seven participants reported that they got their General Education Diploma (GED) prior to applying to college. Three reported that they had gained a high school equivalency diploma through an online procedure (which involved submitting state paperwork, quarterly reports, and any aptitude or achievement testing they took part in). The rest gained admission with no official diploma at all. Seven reported taking the SAT or ACT, others stated that taking these aptitude tests were either not part of the admissions procedure at the undergraduate institution they chose or that they were personally not interested in testing due to their philosophy of education. A majority stated that the most common path to gaining admission to a four-year college was by taking classes at a community college and using those transcripts as a basis for admission. These students also gained college credit that was easily transferred into their four-year undergraduate institution. Many students who chose the community college route chose to enter at a young age (16, most typically) and then proceeded to their four-year college or university between the ages of 16 and 20.

Some of the respondents mentioned interviews and/or portfolios as playing a major role in their college admissions. Others mentioned introducing themselves directly to the dean or coordinator of the major or program they were interested in enrolling in. Many admission officers report seeking homeschoolers and unschoolers, as they tend to be their most creative and self-directed candidates. In an interview with NBC news, Amherst College Dean of Admissions Katie Fretwell stated that homeschoolers and unschoolers tend to have "thicker folders, in a good way" and are "innovative thinkers that bring a lot to the table" (Slater-Tate, 2016). Harvard's Dean of Freshman stated that "we've had a lot of success with students who identify as homeschooled," noting that the definition of homeschooling has changed over time, "so I don't know if you can say these are people who've only gotten their education within the four walls of their home," an apparent nod to more untraditional unschoolers (Tong and Tuysuzoglu, 2017). One respondent shared her path to college:

> When I was 15, I wanted to take community college courses. At that time, dual enrollment of homeschooled students wasn't really accepted, so I was

told I needed to go get my GED to be allowed to enroll. Although I think it disappointed my parents for me to get my GED, it has helped to have that paper that shows I completed some sort of high school education. That said, I refuse to take standardized tests now (because I believe they aren't a measure of intelligence or even what a student has learned), so I did complete my associate's degree before I attempted to transfer to a 4 year university (as some schools will accept a 2 year degree in place of SAT/ACT scores). I graduated from Cornell University with my Bachelors in Psychology. I think unschooling helped me adjust to college; I was so used to being able to study whenever I wanted that it seemed natural to take classes that interested me. And unschooling also follows the premise that if a child has a goal, they'll learn whatever they need in order to meet it; for instance, I don't like math, but I knew I would need to learn it in order to graduate. So that's what I did. (Riley and Gray, 2015)

On the whole, participants reported adjusting to the academic requirements of college well and reported that the benefits of the unschooling outweighed negatives when it came to adjusting to college. The most common advantage cited when asked about adjusting to college had to do with the intrinsic motivation and self-direction they had while unschooling. Many mentioned that going to college was their own choice (and not a parental expectation), therefore they had more internal investment in their work. Others stated that college was much like unschooling in that they got to choose courses and/or a major that they loved. A few participants mentioned that there was a learning curve when it came to formalities, note-taking, and having class at a specific time in college, but indicated that these challenges were quickly surmounted.

Several participants noted that they were surprised at the non-motivation some of their classmates had when it came to college courses and subject matter. Others were hoping to find an intellectually stimulating experience in college and then found out that most of their peers were more interested in drinking, partying, and fraternity or sorority life. Some students specifically chose to find work off-campus or find friends or community off-campus so that their lives weren't limited to just the college campus. As an example:

I was scholarshipped for a large chunk of my undergraduate education due to a portfolio that I assembled and my college interviews. Applying for college didn't seem to be too difficult without an official diploma because I had SAT scores to submit and high school transcripts that my

> mom prepared from all her years journaling our unschooling exploits. I remember being very restless for the first 1 – 2 years of college. I didn't feel very challenged by the core classes I was enrolled in and was itching to move on to my major and minor classes....College was fun but I was stunned to realize that the majority of the other students didn't work or pursue any other area of their lives apart from the studies and partying. I supported myself throughout my four year degree typically working at least 2 jobs while taking well above the minimum class load requirements so that I could graduate on time. Two years into my degree I took a full time job in the creative department of the local newspaper, where I continued to work after graduation. The newspaper I worked for had a scholarship program that helped to pay for one class a semester, so I began working on my liberal arts Master's degree. (Riley and Gray, 2015)

Grown Unschoolers' Employment and Career Choices

The original Gray and Riley (2015) survey asked if participants were currently employed and if those interests matched any activities or interests they pursued as a child or teen. After initial analysis, Gray and Riley went on to send participants a follow-up survey, that asked them to list the paying jobs they held, whether or not they were financially independent, and to describe any additional or future career aspirations or initiatives they had in mind. Eighty-four percent of participants responded to the follow-up questionnaire. With the exception of participants who were full time students and mothers of young children, all respondents were employed. Seventy-eight percent of respondents were earning enough to be financially self-sufficient, and many stated that this was because of the frugality and autonomy they learned while living in an unschooling family. As one participant wrote, "Making a good living is important to me, but my definition of a 'good living' might be different from other people's.... I don't want to be rich. I just want to live joyfully" (Riley and Gray, 2015).

Other major findings of Riley and Gray's research included the fact that most unschooled adults had pursued careers that matched interests they had in their childhood or teenage years. They tended to choose careers that were intrinsically motivating and joyful over potentially more profitable career paths. A majority of respondents had gone into the creative arts (48%) or defined themselves as entrepreneurs (53%) A substantial number, mostly men, had gone into STEM (science, technology, engineering, or math) careers (29%). One will notice that joy is a repeated phrase in discussions of unschooling. The field is filled with testimonies of unschooled individuals discussing the happiness they feel having so much autonomy over their lives, and the excitement that comes with choosing what one wants to learn (Trotman et al., 2018).

Careers Based on Childhood and Teen Interests

Seventy-seven percent of participants in the Gray and Riley (2015) study described a relationship between childhood or adolescent interests and current career path. These careers were seen as meaningful and helpful. As one participant noted "I am currently a freelance sign language interpreter. While unschooling, I studied American Sign Language for years, which gave me the basis for my current profession. I am also a professional ballet dancer, something I studied all my life." Another participant wrote "I run an online craft shop selling craft supplies and jewelry. I am also active as a graphic design and web master. This situation does indeed match with lots of interests I already had as a child." Still another shared, "I am the owner of a construction company. This company is a direct reflection of many of my interests and activities I had as an unschooled youth – for example, democracy in the workplace, environmental stewardship, construction and building, facilitation and project management" (Riley and Gray, 2015).

As with all studies, the Gray and Riley (2015) and Riley and Gray (2015) studies on young adult unschoolers have particular limitations. The most obvious limitation is that the study relied on self-selected data, meaning the unschoolers who responded chose to be in the study and were not a result of random sampling. It may be that the unschoolers who responded did so because they experienced success within an unschooling environment. However, these studies are currently the only peer-reviewed studies on unschooling graduates to date and tell us much about the lives and experiences of those who have unschooled (Lyon, 2018).

One Adult Unschooler's Story

Everyone experiences unschooling differently. Some individuals relish in their experience learning and living within the world. Others may be appreciative of their past but feel they missed out on either the academic aspects of being in school or the social environment that comes with attending public or private school. Unschooling is a choice, one not only made by the parent or family but also by the individual who is being unschooled. The below narrative is one of a twenty-three-year-old who had been unschooled for the entirety of his school career. This is the story of my son, Benjamin Riley.

I was unschooled throughout my school years (K-12th grade). My first day of school was my first day of college. My mother was a young single parent when we started unschooling, and we lived in my grandparent's basement. During the time that we were unschooling, my mom was either working or going to school, and most years, she was doing both. We lived a very simple lifestyle, and my mom would take flexible jobs or teach online courses so she could either be home with me, or take me with her when she was working. Sometimes my grandmother, grandfather, or aunt would watch me while my mom worked. Later on, when I was eleven, my mom got married and we moved into a house. We kept the same basic lifestyle, with my mom working and going to school. At a couple of points during my childhood and adolescence, my mom was working, getting her graduate degrees, and caregiving, as her new husband (who I have always considered to be my dad) got cancer twice. Unschooling certainly did not shelter me from real life issues, and quite honestly, life was sometimes hard. But I am sharing because many times, people see unschooling as something only people with lots of economic resources and "perfect lives" do, and that is just not true.

We (very loosely) used a Waldorf inspired curriculum. However, the curriculum was mainly present to add external legitimacy, as the vast majority of my unschooling journey was interest-based rather than curriculum-based. The contemporary distinctions between 'unschooling' and 'homeschooling' was not something that either myself or my mom attached strict definitions to. Life and learning were (and still are, in my experience) inextricably connected. My mom acted as a kind, loving, and caring facilitator, making sure that I was healthy and safe, but otherwise not lecturing, advising, or interfering unless I asked for assistance. We viewed life and learning as inseparable rather then something that only occurs within the walls of a classroom. As a result, the idea of 'school at home' made absolutely no sense to either myself or my mom, and so we never attempted or even considered it.

I am a professional musician, music educator, writer, editor, and website administrator. I also perform throughout New York and New Jersey as a classical and acoustic guitarist and singer/songwriter, have a rapidly growing private studio of 19 students, and teach music lessons at a local music school. In addition, I am a freelance writer, having written and edited articles for a variety of publications, and also build, design, and administer websites for local entrepreneurs and businesses. My current career evolved from my obsession with playing the guitar, which started at age 13. Within a couple of weeks of taking lessons, I fell in love with the instrument and spent most of my time playing, practicing, and learning as much as possible about the guitar. This enabled me to develop a high level of proficiency on the instrument, paving the way for me to study music at both the undergraduate and graduate level.

I attended Berklee College of Music's Master Guitar Certificate Program from ages 16–18. Upon completion of my studies at Berklee, I attended Nyack College from 2014–2018. Nyack College was the perfect fit for me at the time. It was a small, local college with a good music program. I graduated from Nyack College in 2018 with a Bachelor's of Music in Classical Guitar Performance, Summa Cum Laude, and I am currently a graduate student at Hunter College in New York City, where I am pursuing an M.A. in Music with a concentration in Music Theory. I work several jobs, am a full-time graduate student, and pay my tuition, student loans from undergrad, and the majority of my personal expenses. My long-term goal is to make enough of a living to own a house and have a family while doing work that uses all of my creative talents, is personally meaningful, and makes a positive difference in the lives of others. My ultimate career aspiration is to become a full-time, tenured professor at a reputable university and also continue to teach private lessons, as well as perform both as a solo and ensemble musician.

In my experience, the college application process as an unschooler varies depending on the college. For instance, at Berklee and at Hunter the process was quite smooth. However, the process was more difficult at my undergraduate institution, where the admissions officer at first expressed much skepticism regarding my educational background. This quickly subsided when I sent him my resume and a portfolio of my work. While the transition from unschooling to formal higher education has in many ways been quite smooth, I did experience some challenges along the way. As an unschooler, I was never an avid note taker and had to learn how to take notes on the main points of classes and due dates for assignments, rather than on anything that I happened to find interesting. I also had to work on increasing the neatness of my handwriting, and significantly improve my time management skills. Also, I was not used to studying "for the test". For me, learning has always either been either for its own purpose or as part of achieving a specific goal, usually of my own choosing. I still despise studying "for the test," but I understand that this type of studying is necessary to do well in college. Because I chose to attend college rather than being coerced or forced to attend, I saw these challenges as hoops to jump through that I might not enjoy but were necessary in order to reach a goal of my own choosing.

Everyone asks about socialization. I would say having to answer this question was one of the few downsides of unschooling. It's quite honestly annoying to always answer the question "if you don't go to school, how do you make friends?" I have always had friends of a wide range of ages, backgrounds, ethnicities, cultures, and beliefs. I met most of my friends through simply living life, for instance by running errands, talking with neighbors, going to libraries and museums, and, later, in work contexts as well. I would say that my social life now is similar to my social life as a kid, with the significant positive difference that now most people talk to me as an equal rather than as someone of less importance than them.

The main advantages of unschooling included the ability to learn what I wanted to learn when and how I wanted to learn it, as well as having the time and space to think, explore, and also be bored sometimes. It's okay to be bored. It's healthy and natural. I learned to enjoy my own company as well as the company of others, and this skill has saved me a lot of time, money, and energy, especially as a young adult. I also learned a lot about 'real-world' skills such as budgeting, time management, running errands, and communicating clearly. I am grateful that by being unschooled, I was able to develop strong and genuine relationships with my immediate family. I also developed critical thinking skills and a tendency to question conventional norms when they don't make sense. I had the time and space to extensively explore my interests, which has led me to my current life and career. However, the most important advantage of unschooling is that I learned ***how*** *to learn anything I have or will ever* ***need*** *to learn.*

The main disadvantage of unschooling was having to constantly be questioned (sometimes quite harshly) about it by nearly all of my extended family, neighbors, and local community members, even those I was quite close to. Because of these experiences, one of my favorite things about being an adult is that I can be in public during school hours and no one asks me why I'm not in school! On the flip side, learning to defend an unconventional choice has taught me the importance of standing up for my beliefs and advocating for those who are marginalized and/or oppressed in our society, having once been outside of the mainstream myself.

In unschooling, learning doesn't happen in a straight line, and I have learned some 'simple' skills later on, such as taking notes, writing neatly, and filling out forms. To some, this nonlinear progression may be a disadvantage, but I see it as a normal part of life. As adults, we all have very different skill sets and are constantly learning and adapting as we go along. Here's a novel idea: as adults, we're all unschooling ourselves, but our society has somehow decided that the best way to prepare us for this is to force us, when we are young, to go somewhere where we are trained to obey orders and do what "superiors" say. Then when we become adults, elders become surprised when we have no idea how to live life. I see this experience in many of my traditionally schooled peers, and truly empathize with them. As you might imagine, I think the process of unschooling is MUCH better preparation for 'real life', whatever that is, then sitting in a classroom with a teacher and same age peers.

If I choose to have children, I will most likely unschool or homeschool them. After having known many people who attended public school and after working as a substitute teacher, I have found that more learning happens in an hour of unschooling then in a whole day of public school. Also, as I mentioned above, I think unschooling does a significantly better job preparing children for adult life, and is more enjoyable for the children, parents, and everyone involved. Some of my most treasured moments happened during the time I was unschooled. However, I would ultimately leave that choice up to the child. If they wanted to go to public school or a less traditional school, I would probably allow them to do so.

Unschooling is as much a way of life as it is an educational philosophy. The idea of following your own interests instead of relying on the demands of society for your self-worth and self-concept is nothing short of revolutionary. It has profoundly shaped my worldview, encouraging me to view myself and the world around me from a posture of open-mindedness, creativity, and personal authenticity. Overall, by being unschooled, I learned possibly the most important thing a person can learn: that I have the ability to accomplish and learn whatever I set my mind to do. Life has unlimited possibilities.

References

Cogan, M. (2010). Exploring academic outcomes of homeschooled students. *The Journal of College Admission*. https://files.eric.ed.gov/fulltext/EJ893891.pdf.

Gray, P., & Chanoff, D. (1986). Democratic schooling: What happens to young people who have charge of their own education? *American Journal of Education, 94*(2), 182–213.

Gray, P., & Riley, G. (2013). The challenges and benefits of unschooling, according to 232 families who have chosen that route. *The Journal of Unschooling and Alternative Learning, 7*, 1–27.

Gray, P., & Riley, G. (2015). Grown unschoolers' evaluations of their unschooling experience: Report I on a survey of 75 unschooled adults. *Other Education, 4*(2), 8–32.

Lyon, R. (2018, March 19). Grown unschoolers' evaluation of their unschooling: Report I. *Homeschooling Research Notes*. https://gaither.wordpress.com/2018/03/19/grown-unschoolers-evaluations-of-unschooling-report-i/.

Miedima, L. E. (2016). *Exploring moral character in everyday life: Former democratic school students understandings and school experiences* (MPhil Thesis). University of Brighton, Sussex.

Montes, G. (2015). The social and emotional health of homeschooled students in the United States, a population-based comparison with publicly schooled students based on the National Survey of Children's Health, 2007. *National Home Education Research Institute*, 31. https://www.nheri.org/home-school-researcher-the-social-and-emotional-health-of-homeschooled-students-in-the-united-states-a-population-based-comparison-with-publicly-schooled-students-based-on-the-national-survey-of-child/.

Ray, B. D. (2017). A systematic review of the empirical research on selected aspects of homeschooling as school choice. *Journal of School Choice, 11*, 604–621.

Riley, G., & Gray, P. (2015). Grown unschoolers' experiences with higher education and employment: Report II on a survey of 75 unschooled adults. *Other Education, 4*(2), 33–53.

Slater-Tate, A. (2016, February 11). Colleges welcome growing number of homeschooled students. *NBC News*. https://www.nbcnews.com/feature/college-game-plan/colleges-welcome-growing-number-homeschooled-students-n520126.

Taylor, A. (2020, March 30). Perhaps it's time to consider unschooling. *The Cut*. https://www.thecut.com/2020/03/unschooling-your-kids-during-coronavirus-quarantine.html.

Tong, S. W., & Tuysuzoglu, I. (2017, December 10). From homeschool to Harvard. *The Harvard Crimson*. https://www.thecrimson.com/article/2017/12/10/homeschool-harvard/.

Trotman, D., Lees, H. E., & Willoughby, R. (2018). *Education studies: The key concepts*. London and New York: Routledge.

Webb, J. (2006). The outcomes of home based education: Employment and other issues. *Educational Review, 41,* 121–133.

Westover, T. (2018). *Educated*. New York: Random House.

CHAPTER 10

Branches of Unschooling

There are many different ways to unschool. Some families use their home as a primary learning place. Others spend lots of time in their urban neighborhoods, suburban backyards, or rural farms. Many families unschool on the road, traveling to and from various activities, museums, and historical places. A selected few travel farther, outside their comfort zone and their continent. These unschoolers are called worldschoolers, and are growing in number each and every day. Worldschooling has become so popular, it is becoming an industry, as you can find worldschooling groups, home-sharing websites, conferences, camps, and travel guides easily across the internet.

Worldschooling

Worldschooling can be defined as experiencing the world as one's classroom. It is a form of home education or unschooling where travel takes the place of school. When those within the homeschooling and unschooling communities think of the term worldschooling, all roads lead to its unofficial founder, Lainie Liberti. Lainie is a former corporate branding expert, who, in 2008, left her career to spend more time with her then 9-year-old son, Miro. She closed her business, sold or gave away most of their possessions, and started an adventure that became a lifestyle as well as an educational movement.

G. Riley, *Unschooling*, Palgrave Studies in Alternative Education,
https://doi.org/10.1007/978-3-030-49292-2_10

Worldschooling can be done alone, with family and friends, or more formally through Liberti's program called Project World School. Project World School is a two- to four-week retreat program open to adolescents and young adults ages 13–25. These 2–4 week retreats cost approximately 2500–4000 USD, depending on the location, and include the participant's lodging, food, workshops, attractions, lectures, and classes. The cost of international flights to get to and from the retreat location is not covered. The mission of Project World School is to provide international learning experiences for adolescents and young adults with a strong emphasis on cooperative learning, co-creation, community, and social learning. The retreats themselves focus on offering a deeper cultural immersion that differs from a regular tourist experience. Each retreat offers the opportunity for a past participant to participate as a volunteer in a future retreat, providing teen and young adult participants with intense group facilitation and leadership experience (Lainie Liberti, personal communication, 2017). In 2016, Project World School organized five retreats, serving 40 worldschooling teens and young adults. These trips brought participants to Mexico, the Amazon, Peru, Wales, and Thailand (Riley, 2017). Each year of Project World School brings new locations and new adventures. For example, in 2020, Project World School has trips planned in Europe, Mexico, Japan, Peru, South America, Vietnam, and Thailand.

Project World School attendees experience learning and progress physically, academically, personally, and social emotionally (Ferraro, 2016; Riley, 2017). In Mexico, participants' favorite activities included swimming with turtles in Akumal, climbing and biking around Coba, visiting ruins, and learning about Mayan and Mexican culture. Learning was deep, long-lasting, and relevant within the Amazon Jungle retreat. Participants learned about mycology, botany, conservation, bird behavior, and the history of the Amazon. Participants also reported learning more about self-care and wellness, the importance of hydrating, regular meals, and napping to catch up on sleep. Packing and washing one's own clothes was a life skill learned, as well as the importance of daily meditation and connection with nature. In Peru, participants explored Cusco and the Sacred Valley, and also learned about money conversion, Peruvian art, and weaving. In Wales, farming, beekeeping, and hiking were daily activities, and building a roundhouse was the highlight of the trip. In Thailand, participants were busy learning rock climbing, Muay Thai, Tai Chi, and Qi Gong. They gained knowledge about the power of

Thai prayer, Buddhist and Muslim peoples and cultural practices, batik painting, and Thai household and cultural norms (Riley, 2017).

At the end of each day, Liberti and her son, Miro facilitate circle time. Circle time is an integral part of all Project World School retreats. It is a chance for Project World School participants to reflect deeply on their day and gain information regarding the agenda for the next day. The day's wins, losses, worries, and achievements are also shared. Lainie Liberti generally leads circle time for the first week, and after the first week, any participant who would like to lead circle time can choose to, providing integral facilitation and group leadership experience.

In 2017, I asked Liberti about the benefits of the worldschool experience. She stated:

> Besides the feeling of being connected to one's own internal ability to learn in real time, love of learning is absolutely experienced through world schooling. As an unschooler who worldschools, I can see in real time learning that covers every single academic subject (language, arts, history, science, etc.). I also see so many experiential "soft skills" being honed in through travel. Examples run far and wide….learning patience, teamwork, leadership, service, compassion, critical thinking, problem solving, self-reliance, vast social interaction with people of all ages and walks of life, and being able to have a voice to advocate for oneself. (Personal communication, January 24, 2017)

The challenges of worldschooling were also discussed with Liberti. Major challenges of worldschooling for families include time and cost. A challenge for participants is sometimes fear of exploration and new situations. Another challenge is being tempted to "force" learning during travel, and not realizing that learning happens naturally and organically. The biggest challenge, however, lies in having the outside world see worldschooling as a legitimate form of education. This doubt from the outside world permeates through the self-directed learning community, whether one is unschooling, worldschooling, or attending an unschooling cooperative. Despite this challenge, Project World School and the worldschooling movement is gaining considerable traction as a viable alternative to traditional education. Each and every year, more teens, young adults, and their families register for Project World School retreats or engage in a worldschooling adventure of their own.

Since 2017, Project World School has expanded beyond teen retreats, as Liberti noticed that there was increased interest in families, and not just teens, being able to travel together and worldschool on their own. Liberti and her son, Miro, are now offering Project World Schooling Summits, or international gatherings where families interested in or engaging in world schooling can learn about the benefits and challenges of location independence, traveling with children, and health and wellness on the road. A Virtual Summit, where participants can hear stories of individuals unschooling while traveling, as well as being exposed to different speakers within the home education and worldschooling movement via the internet is also currently being offered. These Summits offer a place where beginning or advanced worldschoolers can share stories and experiences of unschooling or homeschooling while traveling, and their experiences living in specific places. Project World School is also organizing trips for young unschooled adults wanting to experience solo travel, but with the comfort of a group of people to support an individual's solo adventures. This entrepreneurial addition to Project World School is created and managed by Laine's twenty-one-year-old son , Miro (Lainie Liberti and Miro Siegel, personal communication, January 10, 2019).

Of course, there are individuals who worldschool without being involved in Project World School at all. Many have paid their debts, and sold their possessions, houses, and cars so they could have the opportunity to live and learn on the road. Others worldschool through planning trips with their children various times during the year. Websites such as World Schooler Exchange offer listings of long-term house swaps or house rentals for worldschoolers. The site also offers a listing of hosts, pet sitters, work exchanges, and resources for those interested in international learning opportunities specifically for homeschooling and unschooling families or families engaged in some form of alternative learning.

Forest or Outdoor Schooling

One doesn't have to travel far to experience an entirely new world. Sometimes, that world is right in their backyard. Forest or Outdoor schooling is a type of unschooling that is done primarily outside. It is part of a wider educational model that is quite popular in Europe, and has been since the 1800s (Forest School Association, 2020). In the United States, Forest Schooling has been popularized by Richard Louv, author of *Last Child in the Woods: Saving Our Children from Nature Deficit Disorder* (2008), Peter Gray (2013), and Ben Hewitt (2014). Forest or Outdoor

Schooling allows children and teens to spend most of their time in their backyards, or within the farm or forest, learning and growing based on the natural rhythms of nature. Learning within the forest or outdoors also involves much independent and collaborative play. In a study of Forest Schooling in the United Kingdom, Coates and Pimlott-Wilson concluded, "Situating learning within a novel environment, where the traditional boundaries of schooling are stripped away, presented children with the opportunity to not only develop their skill sets, but also reflect on their own educational experiences, transferring their knowledge and understanding between contexts" (2019).

Ben Hewitt was introduced to unschooling, and particularly, forest schooling, in his 20s by observing a father and two sons that lived nearby in Vermont. Sometimes he saw them studying, but most times, the boys were out exploring the woods and the surrounding area. On weekends, they would sell burritos at music festivals, with the boys prepping orders and making change. Ben was immediately drawn to the unschooling lifestyle, full of freedom, autonomy, and real-life skills. Ben's then girlfriend, who later became his wife, was intrigued by the boys too. Inspired by this family, they later decided to unschool their own children, although they prefer the term self-directed learning.

Ben and his wife now live on a 43-acre farm in Vermont with their two sons. Their sons spend most of the day outdoors. As he describes:

> Our days do have structure: chores morning and evening, gardens to be turned and planted, berries to be picked and sold, all these things and so many more repeating in overlapping cycles. But even with these routines, Fin and Rye determine how their days will be spent. Often, they disappear for hours at a time, their only deadline being whichever meal comes next. On their backs, they wear wooden pack baskets that they wove under the tutelage of a friend who also unschools her children. When they return, the baskets are heavy with the small treasures of their world and their heads are full of the small stories of their wandering; the moose tracks they saw, the grouse they flushed, the forked maple they sat beneath to eat snacks. (Hewitt, 2014)

Although not everyone is able to practice Forest or Outdoor schooling, the benefits of this particular learning environment are important to review, both from an overall educational and unschooling perspective. We know that in traditional school environments, taking children and teens out of school to explore their natural surroundings and engage in real-world learning and play is important (Davies et al., 2013). We also know that outdoor learning enhances social-emotional development, intrinsic motivation, increased achievement, and collaborative skills (Coats and Pimlott-Wilson, 2019; Davies et al., 2013; Louv, 2008). For unschoolers, being able to spend time in the outdoors for majority of the day, playing and learning through nature, has innumerable and long-lasting benefits (Louv, 2008).

Hackschooling

Hackschooling is a relatively new term, the brainchild of unschooled teen Logan LaPlante, who delivered a TEDx talk at the University of Nevada entitled "Hackschooling Makes Me Happy." In this talk, with over 10 million views, LaPlante describes his days unschooling, but focuses on his primary motivation: to be healthy and happy. He talks about how mainstream educators don't seem to make personal happiness or health a priority in schools, and calls for the practice to be considered in education (2013).

LaPlante was inspired by Dr. Robert Walsh, a mental health professional who focuses on therapeutic lifestyle changes. Walsh theorizes that eight elements should be prioritized in a person's life for lasting life change, health, and happiness. These elements are exercise, diet and nutrition, time in nature, contribution and service, relationships, recreation, relaxation and stress management, and religious and spiritual practice (Walsh, 2020). LaPlante makes the point that hardly any of these elements are focused on within traditional public schools, stating that "much of education is orientated towards making a living, instead of making a life" (2013).

It is creating a good life that LaPlante wants to focus on, and he does that by unschooling and exploring the world around him. He states that the "hack" in "hackschooling" is not only about taking shortcuts, but also about prioritizing happiness and hacking to change things—even huge things like education. For example, writing goes a lot quicker when you are writing about something you like; and physics becomes more fun (and you get more learning done), when it is focused on activities, experiments, and the study of popular icons such as Newton and Galileo. Subjects don't have to be taught in one year to be taught well. They can be taught in a semester, within a few weeks, or even in a day (2013).

LaPlante says he spends a lot of time in ski resorts and learns greatly from that time. He gains knowledge about weather, snow conditions, geography, and personal safety. He also compares the ski slope to life. He states that instead of everyone skiing the same mountain, we can be creative and do things differently...maybe ski on a different slope. Through taking a different path, we learn unique skills that we can share with others. We can then help one another, using our distinctive skills, enhancing the communities and industries we build together. We can even change education as a whole to make it work for each individual (2013).

Interestingly, LaPlante now attends a flexible, attendance-optional school that is a mix of traditional school, independent projects, and lots of skiing. He knows that unschooling isn't just a type of schooling, but also a mindset. For example, a person can unschool within traditional school as long as they are the ones primarily choosing what they learn, what they want to achieve, how they want to be assessed, if at all, and what they want to do with a majority of their time (Krcmar, 2014).

Unschooling Cooperatives and Self-Directed Learning Centers

Some parents do not have the financial or time-based resources to unschool their child on their own. In this case, parents can choose to participate in an unschooling cooperative. An unschooling cooperative is a place where unschooling families can join together to learn and play. Most unschooling cooperatives are planned by a single family or a few families wanting to unschool their children. They either utilize each other's homes as the "base" for learning, or rent a community space like a library, community center, or basement at a house of worship. Unschooling cooperatives may offer classes based on student interests, or they can just provide an environment where their children can play, learn, and socialize. Many have mission statements, or a list of values or ideas they abide by. Some unschooling cooperatives charge tuition, others are more informal "drop in centers." The Alliance for Self-Directed Education has organized a listing of unschooling cooperatives within their resource directory.

More formal unschooling cooperatives have been formed and are also known as self-directed learning centers. Self-Directed Learning Centers, sometimes identified as freeschools, generally follow the philosophy of A. S. Neill, and focus on the right of the child or teen to choose their own educational path guided by interests and strengths. In freeschools, there is no one-up, one-down, or teacher/student relationship. Instead, adults serve as resources, facilitators, or partners in learning. Students within freeschools create their own curriculum or schedule their own day. They also organically work on things like life construction (solving the problems inherent in life), socialization, creating a personal identity, and moral, spiritual, or ethical development (Valeev and Valeeva, 2013).

One of the most well-known self-directed learning centers for middle and high school teens is called North Star, in Sunderland, Massachusetts. North Star was founded by Ken Danford and Joshua Hornick in 1996. Previously, Danford and Hornick both worked as public middle school teachers. North Star is a true unschooling-inspired self-directed learning center. It provides classes in many different topics of interest based on the needs of their students, but attendance at those classes are optional. Examples of current class offerings include: The Election of 2020, Jewelry Making, How To Listen to Classical Music, Anatomy 101, American Sign Language and Deaf Culture, Social Science Research Design and Debates, and Empathic Intelligence. North Star also finds internships, work experiences, or volunteer opportunities for its members if that is how they choose to spend their days. North Star's mission centers on the idea that school is optional and that teens don't have to wait until they "grow up and graduate" to live the life they want. As Ken Danford states in his book *Learning Is Natural, School Is Optional*, "My job is helping people believe in themselves, and to believe there is a space for them in society. I know that school is optional, and I understand that many people have found success in many ways, independent of their school experiences or credentials" (2019).

Inspired by North Star, The Princeton Learning Cooperative (PLC), founded by former social studies teacher Joel Hammon, is another successful example of a large unschooling cooperative serving teens in the Princeton, New Jersey area. PLC is focused on an adolescents' strengths and interests, providing them opportunities, support, and one on one mentoring. Staff at PLC work with students to create their own individual goals and a plan for achieving those goals. PLC works under the guiding principles that young people naturally want to learn, that school is not required to do this, and that learning happens everywhere. PLC has been so successful that two other learning cooperatives have opened under its umbrella—the Bucks Learning Cooperative in Pennsylvania and the Raritan Learning Cooperative in Flemington, New Jersey (Hammon, 2016).

As the unschooling movement grows, new and different ways to unschool continue to be created. Children and teens learn in many different ways, and it is clear that the traditional classroom is not always the optimal (or only) environment in which learning happens. Worldschoolers learn through travel. Forest or Outdoor Schoolers learn through interaction with the environment, and Hackschoolers learn not only how to take "learning shortcuts," but also how to create optimal physical, social, and emotional learning environments for themselves. For those families where traditional unschooling is not an option, or for children or teens who need a community of learners to thrive, there are learning cooperatives and self-directed learning centers to consider. These environments allow students to take control of their own learning (and life) within supportive individual and group settings.

References

Alliance for Self-Directed Education (ASDE). (2020). https://www.self-directed.org/.

Coates, J. K., & Pimlott-Wilson, H. (2019). Learning while playing: Children's Forest School experiences in the UK. *British Education Research Journal, 45*, 21–40.

Danford, K. (2019). *Learning is natural, school is optional*. Sutherland, MA: Golden Door Press.

Davies, D., Jindal-Snape, D., Collier, C., Digby, R., Hay, P., & Howe, A. (2013). Creative learning environments in education—A systematic literature review. *Thinking Skills and Creativity, 8*, 80–91.

Ferraro, A. (2016). Evaluation of a temporary, immersive learning community based on worldschooling. *Journal of Unschooling and Alternative Learning, 10*, 1–12.

Forest School Association. (2020). https://www.forestschoolassociation.org/.

Gray, P. (2013). *Free to learn: Why unleashing the instinct to play will make our children happier, more self reliant, and better students for life*. New York: Basic Books.

Hammon, J. (2016). *The teacher liberation handbook: How to leave school and create a place where you and young people can thrive*. Langhorne, PA: The Grelton Group.

Hewitt, B. (2014, August 12). We don't need no education. *Outside Magazine*. https://www.outsideonline.com/1928266/we-dont-need-no-education.

Krcmar, S. (2014, October 7). The hackschooler goes back to school, sort of. *Outside Magazine*. https://www.outsideonline.com/1926276/hackschooler-goes-back-school-sort.

LaPlante, L. (2013). *Hackschooling makes me happy* [video]. TED Conferences. TEDX at University of Nevada. https://www.youtube.com/watch?v=h11u3vtcpaY.

Louv, R. (2008). *Last child in the woods: Saving our children from nature deficit disorder*. Chapel Hill, NC: Algonquin Books.

North Star. (2020). http://www.northstarteens.org/.

Princeton Learning Cooperative. (2020). https://princetonlearningcooperative.org/.

Riley, G. (2017). Worldschooling: Homeschooling away from home. *International Journal of Education, 9,* 186–191.

Valeev, A. A., & Valeeva, L. A. (2013). Free education: Pro and contra. *Procedia – Social and Behavioral Sciences, 144,* 66–69.

Walsh, R. (2020). *Integral Health Resources*. http://www.integralhealthresources.com/about/.

World Schooler Exchange. (2020). http://worldschoolerexchange.com.

CHAPTER 11

Unschooling Growth and Next Steps

There is a national conversation focusing on educational reform. How do we make schools better? How do we provide learning environments that work for all children? How do we create schools dedicated to equity, diversity, and inclusion? What about grades? What about standardized testing? Are there best practices that work for all students? Does a model exist that works for individuals that may not fit in within the traditional school environment? The answer may lie in looking at aspects of unschooling.

Assessment and the Opt Out Movement

Unschoolers know that assessment does not mean testing or raw data. Unschoolers instead see assessment as coming from a place of true understanding or mastery. Interestingly, schools are beginning to see this too. Numerous researchers and educational policymakers have called for changes in the assessment of public school students, noting that the focus on standardized testing decreases motivation, conflicts with best academic practices, costs extra money, and leads to high rates of teacher dissatisfaction (Cizek and Burg, 2006; Kohn, 2000; Kozol, 2005; Ravitch, 2013). The National Opt Out Movement cites this research, and calls for greater focus on educational reform, starting with a focus on standardized testing. The Opt Out movement has provided a space and forum for teachers, parents, and students to formally "opt out" from state tests (Kirylo,

G. Riley, *Unschooling*, Palgrave Studies in Alternative Education,
https://doi.org/10.1007/978-3-030-49292-2_11

2018). The Opt Out movement has grown tremendously in recent years, despite pushback from state departments of education, local boards of education, and school administrators. Parents (and students) have realized that they now have some control over how they are assessed and data tracked, and this has given them a powerful voice. Rethinking and sometimes refusing ways students are assessed is something unschoolers have always done, and now the mainstream population is thinking about it too (Kirylo, 2018).

Rethinking Learning

Once stakeholders rethink assessment, they rethink learning. Learning becomes not only about the score, the test, or the grade. The conversation shifts. What is real learning? How do students learn best? How do we utilize students' natural strengths and interests within the classroom? How do we create more engaged, intrinsically motivated students? (Abeles, 2016). Unschoolers have been asking these questions all along and now schools are following the lead. Two notable examples of public schools that have changed their thinking about how students learn is Monument Mountain Regional High School in Great Barrington, Massachusetts and High Tech High School in San Diego, California.

Monument Mountain Regional High School and the Independent Project

It was Sam Levin, a student at Monument Mountain, who started the conversation about a new type of school. He looked around at his own classmates, saw disinterest and disengagement, and felt that same way in himself. They (and he) felt unchallenged and unmotivated in their classes. Classwork and homework was completed to please others, namely teachers, but did nothing to motivate students. Levin talked to his mom about this, and she suggested he do something about it. That led to a discussion with his guidance counselor, Mike Powell, about starting a school within a school, focused on project-based, intrinsically motivated learning (Abeles, 2016).

Administration agreed to support the endeavor, and Levin became a student, and Powell the faculty advisor, for the Independent Project at Monument Mountain High School. The project was structured so that students gained academic instruction in core subject areas in the morning. This academic instruction was guided by student questions, and was not direct lesson planned instruction. The afternoon focused on students creating an individual project or endeavor based upon their own internal motivations and passions. One student, for example, focused on writing a book of poetry and short stories. Another student was dedicated to becoming proficient in piano. At the end of the semester, students showcased their knowledge and projects in 20–30 minute presentations to interested students, faculty, and parents. These presentations demonstrated not only students' deep appreciation for their own learning, but also for the learning of their peers, based on the care and encouragement shown to their peers during the showcase.

Within the last three weeks of the project, students were involved in what the Independent Project called a collective endeavor. One semester, when Mike Powell was advising, students decided to create a project centered on educational reform and created a documentary about the Independent Project. One of the biggest learnings that came from creating this documentary was the power of resources, both monetary and human. Students learned to seek resources and funding from their own school, and later on, their community. They gained knowledge regarding not only how to ask for financial resources, but also how to ask non-related adults for information, support, and skill sharing.

Powell shared that because there were no grades associated with these final projects, students were more motivated to heavily invest in them. They felt free to take risks and to make mistakes, and spent time thinking about how to fix those mistakes. In the long run, students also became better problem solvers, were more apt to ask for help later on in their academic careers, and were more thoughtful about their life choices within the realms of college, career, and relationships. Teachers who worked with the Independent Project also gained knowledge about self-directed education, and that understanding reframed their ideas about what education truly could become. After the Project, teachers recognized that learning was not all about direct instruction or leading a class. Instead, education was sometimes about knowing how to work collaboratively with individuals of all ages. Teachers saw a transformation in their role. Instead of being the directors of student learning, they became facilitators and supporters of student learning. Teachers became more protective of student initiative and motivation, instead of being focused on grades and scores. The Independence Project not only changed students and teachers, but had a transformational effect on administrators and school leaders as well (Currie-Knight and Riley, 2019).

One Period a Day

The Independence Project has influenced many educators to try a similar format within their own schools. David Lane was one of those educators. Lane is a public high school teacher who also ran his own self-directed learning center called Ingenuity Hub. During his years teaching public school, Lane picked up Grace Llewellyn's *Teenage Liberation Handbook* (1991) and started thinking about the power of independent, self-motivated learning. He liked the idea of adults being not teachers, but coaches, facilitators, or sources of support for children and teens. He convinced administrators at the traditional high school he was teaching at to give him one period per day where students could do anything they wanted, and they agreed on that one period (David Lane, personal communication, December 27, 2019).

Some students used that one period as "chill out time." Lane was understanding of this, knowing that sometimes students need time and space to sort out things. Being a teenager is hard, and the social-emotional learning that comes from having a break within a day was sometimes more valuable than any academic learning that happens at school. Others chose the time to work on personal projects that were meaningful to them. Lane tells the story of one student, whose father had died during the semester he was enrolled in Lane's self-directed learning class. At first, that student, expectedly, used that time to decompress from a hectic school day and mourn his dad. But then, he shared with Lane that he was ready to work on a project. Specifically, he wanted to build a surfboard, as his dad was interested in surfing and always wanted to work at a surf shop.

The student started working. He spent some time at a surf shop and collected enough money to start creating a surfboard. He drew out a plan. He learned about flotation and density. He experimented with materials, including fiberglass. He wasn't able to make a surfboard but instead made a skimboard. Due to the mixing of the chemicals and materials he used, the skimboard was smelly and non-attractive. The student was upset and was convinced that he failed. But then he showed it to Lane, who had a different view.

Lane asked about the planning, materials, and chemicals used to create the board. The student was able to identify why the skimboard wouldn't do what it was supposed to and talked about the incorrect measurements of chemicals used to finish and cure the skimboard. The student could clearly explain why the board didn't work. To Lane, the board was the greatest success of the class, and he expressed this to the student. Learning is all about making mistakes and trying new things. Through creating the board, the student learned about engineering, chemistry, and math. It's not always (and many times not ever) a beautiful final project that indicates success and mastery. Many times, learning is all about the process. Lane still has that board, keeping it as an example of one of the ultimate successes of his one period per day independent learning program (Lane, personal communication, December 27, 2019).

High Tech High School

Administrators and faculty at High Tech High School, in San Diego, California, realize that learning is all about the process. High Tech High School looks like a different environment for learning. Spaces are open, and students are all around, not just relegated to classrooms. High Tech is a project-based school, dedicated to four specific design principals. These principals are equity, personalization, authentic work, and collaborative design (High Tech High School, 2020).

Equity at High Tech means creating a diverse community of students. Students are admitted on a zip code-based lottery, ensuring that students from all neighborhoods in the San Diego area get an equal chance at attending the high school. There is no academic tracking and no segregation of students in any form. Personalization of learning is key to High Tech's success. Much like an unschooling environment, High Tech focuses on the different gifts and strengths of each student enrolled. Students pursue their passions through projects, and learning is reflection focused. Families are invited to be as involved in the students learning processes as much or as little as they want to be (High Tech High School, 2020). This provides the focus on engaging families and communities that all schools aspire to.

Authentic work is another main principle of High Tech High School. This means that students, much like unschoolers, only engage in work that is meaningful and interesting to them. Students engage in real-world learning through fieldwork experiences and partnerships within their communities. Internships give students a chance to work outside the school, creating an environment for maintenance and generalization of academic learning. Collaborative design is the last principle of High Tech High. At High Tech, teachers act as facilitators and mentors. They do not direct or control the students' learning (High Tech High School, 2020). It took a little while for parents and the community to embrace High Tech High's untraditional approach but once they did, enrollment soared (Abeles, 2016).

Democratic or Sudbury Schooling

As self-directed forms of education are becoming more common, a growing number of Sudbury Schools are being created both in the United States and overseas (Valeeva and Kasimova, 2015). Sudbury model schools allow students of elementary and secondary school age to take full charge of their own education in a democratic environment, where students and staff vote on all school rules (Sadofsky and Greenberg, 1994). This is very much unlike the culture at traditional public schools, where hired administration runs the school, and students follow a set curriculum that they are frequently tested on. As evolutionary psychologist Peter Gray states, "To understand the (Sudbury) school, one has to begin with a completely different mindset from that which dominates current educational thinking. One has to begin with the thought: Adults do not control children's education; children educate themselves" (2008).

Sudbury schools place no academic requirements on students, nor any academic standards for graduation. Students shape their day through being involved in their own personal interests and intrinsic motivations. Staff facilitate and mentor when asked but do not suggest or create activities for students to engage in (Gray and Chanoff, 1986). Public high school English teacher Christine Traxler calls it "the only education model in the United States that affords opportunity for students to fully internalize self trust and autonomy" (Traxler, 2015, p. 271).

As I walk into Hudson Valley Sudbury School (HVSS) on a visit, I feel this self-trust and autonomy permeating through the school. The school itself feels more like a home. There is a kitchen, a gathering space, a library, an art room, a room for playing and recording music, lots of outdoor play spaces, and a room dedicated to meetings and the judicial committee, a hallmark of democratic education. Students are engaged in activities they choose, and adults are there to provide support, if needed or wanted, and to serve as a resource. Hudson Valley Sudbury students are responsible for their spaces, as well as for their behavior. It feels much like an unschooling environment.

According to Matt Gioia, admissions director at HVSS, children and teens are involved in all sorts of activities during the day. More casual activities include laughing and hanging out, recording videos for Instagram or TikTok, playing music, journaling, reading, playing outside, or working on their college applications. There are some organized activities, which have been requested by students, including a weekly class on oriental medicine, a board game club, and a debate club. One group of students have started a small catering business during breakfast and lunch times, providing meals for other students to purchase. Other students provide care to the babies and toddlers that frequently visit the school. School rooms are maintained and cleaned by the students and staff at several points during the day, just like a family would stop to clean a house or play space. School governance is a huge part of the Sudbury philosophy. All rules are democratically created and enforced, and a law book is created and maintained. If a school rule is broken, the HVSS judicial committee investigates and charges the students as necessary. Trials are rare at HVSS, but if a student disagrees with a charge, a trial can occur. The purpose of the democratic structure within the Sudbury School is to have students better understand and participate in democratic structures within life (Currie-Knight and Riley, 2019).

Because Sudbury schools give students extensive freedom to do as they please, the school itself is seen as highly experimental. Similar to apprehensions people have toward unschooling, many are concerned about whether Sudbury schools truly prepare students for academic, career, and personal success in later life. However, Gray and Chanoff's (1986) study on the alumni of Sudbury Valley School in Massachusetts found that Sudbury alumni had no difficulty adjusting to later academic demands and were successful in a wide variety of careers. Gray et al. (2020) are in the middle of similar study of Hudson Valley Sudbury School graduates, to see if Gray and Chanoff's conclusions also relate to smaller, newer Sudbury models.

Focus on Social-Emotional Learning

There are numerous commonalities between more structured unschooling-like school environments and unschooling itself. In both environments, one can observe lots of intrinsically motivated, self-determined learning. Experimental schools like the Independent Project,

David Lane's one period a day experiment and High Tech High School also allowed students some semblance of free choice in activity, so that students had autonomy over some part or all of their day. Most of all, these schools recognized that learning is not just an activity that happens between 8 a.m. and 3 p.m., at desks, in classrooms, using textbooks and workbooks as primary resources. They appreciated that learning happened all the time, in varied supportive environments.

Notably, each school leader also mentioned the social-emotional benefits of self-directed learning. At Monument Mountain Regional High School, home of the Independent Project, students enrolled in the program showed more interest in learning, and seemed happier and more self-assured as a result of their experience (Abeles, 2016). In David Lane's self-directed learning class, a student had time and space to mourn the loss of his father, and then was able to channel that sadness into a project that connected him to his dad (David Lane, personal communication). At High Tech High School, students are not tracked or divided, but acknowledged for the strengths and gifts they bring to the table (High Tech High School, 2020). At Hudson Valley Sudbury School, children and teens have the time and space to explore not only the things they are interested in, but also their emotions, and their role within the community and greater world. Social-emotional learning is an essential part of each of these communities, each and every day. It is not taught through curriculum, or learned through workbooks or journals. Instead, it was a lived and nurtured experience.

Unfortunately, with the exception of High Tech High School and Hudson Valley Sudbury School, some of these experimental school communities don't exist anymore. Changes in administration made sustaining self-directed spaces within public high schools an impossibility. Funding was identified as a constant source of stress. Finding a consistent group of students (and parents) who bought in to the idea of a self-directed learning environment within a traditional school structure proved to be challenging. Unless there is whole school- and district-based support for spaces like these, and a body of research that supports the benefits of intrinsically motivated learning within traditional schools, sustainability will always be a struggle.

The Future of Schools

Just as people are multidimensional, education is too. It never will be one size fits all. Children learn in all different ways, and the traditional classroom is not the right environment for everyone. Unschooling is a choice, just like homeschooling, public schooling, private schooling, and charter schooling. Thirty years ago, those who were unschooling did so mostly in secret. Today, people view unschooling as a growing educational movement, as they observe the benefits of intrinsically motivated, self-directed learning.

If Sir Ken Robinson (2006) is correct, the future of school reform is rooted in the unschooling movement. However, schools need to be able to let go of preexisting structures and expectations that are, quite obviously, not working in their favor. In order to change, schools need to do so from the bottom up, rethinking the notion of what education and learning really is. They need to ask the question "what is the purpose of school?" and answer that question with innovative and open minds.

Teachers must be exposed not only to the works of Rousseau and Dewey, but also to the writings of Bowlby, Deci, Ryan, Gardner, Neill, Illich, Holt, and Gray. They need a deep understanding of why schools were created, in order to figure out how to change the structure and function of schools to more deeply meet the needs of students in the twenty-first century. Teacher educators need to be taught not only about the power of extrinsic motivators in the classroom, but also about the potential of intrinsic motivation. Positive behavior supports must be replaced by more restorative, authentic behavioral practices that center on listening deeply to students and their needs. Teachers need to release the notion that they are directors of learning, and discover how they can be facilitators and supporters of self-direction in their students.

Similarly, students need to personally experience the joy and internal motivation that comes from self-directed learning. They need to be given time and space within the school day to process their responsibilities, emotions, and knowledge. They need to be able to make mistakes and grow from them without the high-stakes weight of grades and assessments. They need to be accepted and loved exactly as they are, not only by their peers but also by the adults around them. The classifications and labels we put on students need to be replaced with the notion that all people possess a wide variety of strengths and weaknesses. The secret is to utilize the strengths. Children and teens need to feel true competence in themselves and their ideas. Students need less specific subject direct instruction and more facilitation around how to learn and utilize resources. They need more exposure to the outside world, and more interaction with community members and leaders. They need to know how to generalize their knowledge, so that they can be productive, interactive, and caring members of society at large.

Schools and mindsets need to shift. But until they do, individuals need to be aware of and open to other options. Although not every family, child, or teen will be able to unschool in the traditional sense, they can take the tenets of unschooling and utilize them in whatever environment they find themselves in. They can also utilize the resources found in a growing number of self-directed learning centers to be able to gain knowledge in the way that they choose. Additionally, students can, after a day in traditional school, intentionally use the time they do have to create a self-directed learning program of their own. There are many ways to unschool, and it is my hope that young people find the way that works for them. Unschooling, and exploring learning beyond the traditional classroom, is indeed the future of education. The time to embrace it is now.

References

Abeles, V. (2016). *Beyond measure: Rescuing an overscheduled, overtested, underestimated generation*. New York: Simon and Schuster.

Cizek, G. J., & Burg, S. S. (2006). *Addressing test anxiety in a high-stakes environment: strategies for classrooms and schools*. Thousand Oaks, CA: Corwin Press.

Currie-Knight, K., & Riley, G. (2019–Present). *Learning by living*. https://www.spreaker.com/show/learning-by-living-podcast.

Gray, P. (2008, August 13). *Children educate themselves IV: Lessons from Sudbury Valley*. Retrieved on December 14, 2018 from https://www.psychologytoday.com/us/blog/freedom-learn/200808/children-educate-themselves-iv-lessons-sudbury-valley.

Gray, P., & Chanoff, D. (1986). Democratic schooling: What happens to young people who have charge of their own education? *American Journal of Education, 94*(2), 182–213.

Gray, P., Riley, G., Currie-Knight, K., Puga, L., & Pretty, L. (2020–In progress). *A study of graduates of Hudson Valley Sudbury School*.

High Tech High School. (2020). https://www.hightechhigh.org/about-us/.

Hudson Valley Sudbury School. (2020). https://sudburyschool.com.

Kirylo, J. D. (2018, August 24). The opt out movement and the power of parents. *Phi Delta Kappan*. https://kappanonline.org/kirylo-opt-movement-power-parents/.

Kohn, A. (2000). *The case against standardized testing: Raising the scores, ruining the schools*. Portsmouth, NH: Heinemann.

Kozol, J. (2005). *The shame of the nation: The restoration of apartheid schooling in America*. New York, NY: Three Rivers Press.

Llewellyn, G. (1991). *The teenage liberation handbook: How to quit school and get a real-life education*. Eugene, OR: Lowry House.

Ravitch, D. (2013). *Reign of error: The hoax of the privatization movement and the danger to America's public schools*. New York, NY: Knopf.

Robinson, K. (2006, February). *Ken Robinson: How school kills creativity* [Video file]. Retrieved from http://www.ted.com/talks/ken_robinson_says_schools_kill_creativity.html.

Sadofsky, M. (Ed.), & Greenberg, D. (1994). *Kingdom of childhood: Growing up at a Sudbury Valley School*. Framingham, MA: Sudbury Valley Press.

Sudbury Valley School. (2018). https://sudburyvalley.org/.

Traxler, C. (2015). The most democratic school of them all: Why the Sudbury model of education should be taken seriously. *Schools: Studies in Education, 12*(2), 271–296. Retrieved on December 14, 2018 from https://www.journals.uchicago.edu/doi/full/10.1086/683220.

Valeeva, R. A., & Kasimova, R. S. (2015). Alternative education system Sudbury Valley as a model for reforming school. *Social and Behavioral Sciences, 182*, 274–278.

Index

G. Riley, *Unschooling*, Palgrave Studies in Alternative Education, https://doi.org/10.1007/978-3-030-49292-2

Printed by Printforce, the Netherlands